LYONEL FEININGER

Text by T. Lux Feininger

Photographs by Andreas Feininger

CITY AT THE EDGE OF THE WORLD

Frederick A. Praeger · *Publishers*

New York · Washington · London

BOOKS THAT MATTER

Published in the United States of America in 1965
by Frederick A. Praeger, Inc., Publishers
111 Fourth Avenue, New York 3, N.Y.

Copyright 1965 in Munich, Germany, by Rütten & Loening Verlag GmbH
Library of Congress Catalog Card Number: 65-25280

Printed in Germany

Feininger In der Stadt am Ende der Welt FREITAG d. 12. VII. 1912

It has never been easy to classify the art of Lyonel Feininger. In the early years of his public appearance as a painter, the time before the First World War, he shared the glory and the opprobrium, which then attached equally (at least in Germany) to the quality of the "modern painter," with others not too unlike him. The common aim then was to renew the language of painting, to break with the cult of atmospheric surface values, to re-introduce a spiritual quality into art which it had lost. In those early times, the visual means used by him were amongst the most daring, the most "abstract," if the quality abstracted from is the preoccupation with academic standards, seasoned by a dash of Impressionism. Even then, he was remarkable for his individual ways, essentially already a lonely figure. He did not belong to a movement or to a "school." Later, at the Bauhaus, it was possible for him to be as active and, upon the whole, as happy as was the case, because the Bauhaus was not a "movement"; because, despite the insistence on "collectivism," determination on the part of himself and his colleagues was strong to respect each other's individuality and to resist all attempts to compel the "masters" to espouse artistic and educational doctrines. His membership in the "Blue Four" was founded on similar rights and limitations. His attitude regarding the relation of the artist to his art was always, as he expressed it himself, "at pains to retire behind the work." As the trend in modern art was increasingly in the opposite direction, he found himself more and more alone.

This trend, although difficult to sum up in a few words, is evinced through the variations of the approach of the artist toward "subject-matter." The development—or the decay—of modern painting is marked by certain stages, for which such headings as description, interpretation, transcription, translation, transformation, might serve to characterize a gradually shifting attitude of the artist. The interest moves farther and farther away from the object, the "Thou" of the dialogue (as Paul Klee expressed it); as it does so, it approaches, first, the work itself, the painting or the sculpture, giving it life and importance which are waxing as the concern with the objective "truths" (Ruskin) are waning. To put it a little crudely: as the art of painting declines, "art" and "painting" prosper. For this stage of a

broad, historical process, the proper word is "Expression" and hence, "Expressionism," a term which somehow suited painting in Germany better than it did French painting. "Fauves" and "Cubists" pursued analogous aims insofar as they sought pictorial laws to replace the laws of optics. The visual means of the "Futurists," while strikingly related in certain cases to the means of cubism, were overshadowed in significance by the insistence on dynamic motion, violence, glorification of the dangerous life, briefly, on moral qualities as opposed to visual ones. With the advent of the war, the historical process quickens. Social criticism and a deep disillusionment with the progress of civilization find expression in works still further reducing the importance of visible objects as compared to the importance the artist attaches to the idea of what he is painting. Aesthetic and lyrical qualities of the work are now on the wane, and the views of their creator become the essential criteria. These comprise political, religious, sociological opinions, to which must be added psychological fads and phobias. The coming of the Second World War does not alter the process, merely helps to accelerate it. Throughout, one finds that the "I" of the painter, the subject, gains the importance which the "Thou" continues to lose. The artist thus assumes more and more the role of a messiah, of a preacher, a prophet, an agitator. This function, whether self-styled or assigned to him by an ever-growing critical literature, expresses itself in our time through visual means which are often deliberately chaotic. And the longer one follows this evolution, the more familiar one becomes with such unpainter-like terms as "universal sickness," "crime against humanity," "general destruction." One is at liberty to see a new humanism growing, in this concern with the way humankind is dealing with the Universe; but the criteria of

8

an art which never gave up dealing with the "Thou," conceding it a degree of objective reality, are not covered by such a critique.

The art of Lyonel Feininger is of this kind. Access to it is gained through studying the dialogue between the artist, the "I," and the world around him, the "Thou." A figurative painter, he nonetheless shows a pervading awareness of, and sensitivity toward, the dual nature of reality. His personality is determined by intuition and by will. The latter, so characteristic of his painterly credo, insists on clarity and the unsentimental language of form. These are the products of rigorous self-discipline and great knowledge. At certain phases of his *œuvre* they are apt almost to hide his experience of the *descensus ad inferos*. But—and this is perhaps the main purpose of my study—without the subjective note of intuition, the constructive part of this art would remain intellectual, cold. In my attempt to establish a total view of the artist I shall try to show how fantasy and objectivity, in toys no less than in pictures, interact in the sense of constantly complementing one another. It will be my aim to demonstrate that the work of the artist, seen as a whole, has the function of seeking, of exploring, and of reconciling the dualism of existence.

A critical appreciation of a famous father is a task not lightly to be undertaken. At least for a period, every father is a great man to his son. This happy time is normally followed by another, when youth becomes critical of old age, and the examination is not always followed by appreciation. A too subjective approach is to be shunned. Forearmed with this knowledge, I have tried to make use of a variety of sources of a contrasting nature: the works themselves, letters of my father's to my mother and to myself, and my own memories. The interplay of these sources produces first and foremost a very marked sense of the flow of *time*. There is an ebb as well as a floodtide in this movement: like a novel by Joseph Conrad, the mind is moving in opposing directions. Thinking of my father, I cannot for long avoid being aware of *his* father (whom I have never known); nor can I exclude for any appreciable length of time my consciousness of my having become a father of sons (whom he was never to know) in my turn. I doubt whether I should have ventured to write on the toys without having been able to participate in, to relive, that happy era in which play with toys is all-important and, at the same time, to observe it. It was thus possible, now to remember and anon to forget—whichever seemed proper for

the purpose–that one was a child oneself, to whom all toys were "to play with." Such is the golden privilege of youth. But to the father, especially if he is an artist, play itself is susceptible of various readings. It is not necessarily confined to children. Nor need the toys be of necessity designed for the young. They may, or they may not be; or they may address themselves to the "young in heart." They may have their origin in such a heart.

The toys an artist has fashioned may serve to gain an insight into the formal ideas of their creator. If I consider, for instance, four artists who have made playthings (three of whom I have known personally), I find it impossible to draw a dividing line between "play" and "serious work." The "real work" of each one of them has a play-like grace and ease, and in the "toys" we find enough seriousness to remind us of the gravity of children at play. Paul Klee, Pablo Picasso, Alexander Calder, and Lyonel Feininger, even if they had not all been fathers or whether or not the playful things they have created were destined to be played with and wrecked by children, would all have made excursions into this gamesome world. And they would not have been conscious of crossing any particular boundary in so doing.

The subject-matter of Lyonel Feininger's toys closely parallels that which constitutes his serious work. Ships, trains, houses, and people, with the accessories of bridges, mills, and gaunt trees, is the repertoire of the toys, and in a purely descriptive sense these are also the objects of his attention in painting. However, before a discussion of the handling of these themes can be begun, it is necessary to examine the state of mind in which the artist has approached his work.

Paul Klee, in his essay "Ways of Nature Study," has underlined as characteristic of the art of today its awareness of space; the artist begins his studies with a "spatial image" of the object, be it plant, animal or man, within the spaces of a house, a landscape or the cosmos." The eye is "the meeting place for all ways of nature study," Klee continues, insisting at the same time that the "two ways of humanizing the object (the one of common, earth-bound roots, the other of cosmic kinship) are in their nature 'non-optical.'" This refers to the need for reducing the importance of the surface appearance of objects in the total pictorial concept; reducing, not excluding. Klee is not saying that the painter of today should be blind. Lyonel Feininger attached a similar importance to space in painting, with his personal note of insisting on the value of the element of "nostalgia" or "longing" super-added; an effort of the soul, which leads to the discovery of a consonance of sky, earth, water, man-made objects–*landscape*–which strikes the beholder suddenly as significant; and this significance is so intense that, in

Lyonel Feininger in 1896
with ship model he was building
at the time (unknown)

The artist with his three sons,
summer 1912
(Julie Feininger)

The "old Norwegian Bark" (p. 111)
at the quay at Osternothafen;
the artist in the foreground
summer 1910 (Julie Feininger)

Lyonel Feininger
on the Rega at Deep, 1927
(T. Lux Feininger)

Model yachts in a rough sea
(T. Lux Feininger)

Model yachts in a swell
in calm weather
(T. Lux Feininger)

The beach at Deep
(Lyonel Feininger)

Views of train models of 1914

The artist and a friend, admiring the locomotive of the narrow-gauge railroad between Treptow a. d. R. and Ost-Deep, summer 1933 (Werner Jackson)

experiencing it, one cannot say whether it has created, or is created by, the state of mind. The true subject-matter of his painting is thus exactly this particular consonance (a musical term, by the way) of light and space which ennobles and hallows the humblest object. The state of mind in which it is revealed is therefore in itself the goal of a continuous search. This quest partakes in its nature of the quality of the religious. It is not too much to say that the light which informs Lyonel Feininger's work is expression of an inner light as much as it is a translation into visual terms of an outer atmospheric event.

These remarks refer to his use of color. For structure, no other aspect of his art is more illuminating than his dealing with proportion. From his youth on, he not only showed the keenest sense of the interrelationship of dimensions–height, width, depth, and their respective measurements–but of the expressive meaning of them. In his faculty for appreciating proportion he owned the equipment necessary for the classical artist intent on the pursuit of Ideal Form. But this states less than half the truth of his artistic message, for what law he does not observe, what rule he disregards, is perhaps even more characteristic of the work. Nothing will give a better example than to describe his handling of perspective. In his early cartooning days he had already "broken with perspective" to use his own words. But this "break" is so typical of the subtle mixture of observing and disregarding of rules, that it deserves a little analysis.

Aware of perspective, intellectually comprehending its laws while emotionally sensing that they must be reformulated and adapted to more pressing needs; accepting, or better, insisting on, the principle of distortion but refusing to submit to the restricting factor of fixed location in space of the spectator– thus, possibly, the problem might have presented itself to the artist. In this shorthand description the key lies in the words "location in space." Form, to the artist, means both "true" and "expressive." Since these two qualities are irreconcilable, the solution is found in "distortion of true form." Perspective likewise predicates distortion; but in the academic sense, based on the science of optics, it is treated as a necessary evil, limited to a minimum by means of establishing a fixed point in space (the point of site) and relating all shapes falling within the field of vision dominated by the angle of vision (usually 30 degrees or slightly less) to this point. This procedure is based on the assumption derived from physiology that this field can be surveyed without moving the eye. The inevitable outcome of this method is, of course, to compel the spectator of the perspective image to assume a position analogous to the point of site of the construction, which is merely another way of saying that the beholder's location in space is fixed for him in advance. The purest form of this spectator-image relationship is the

Renaissance invention of the peep-hole perspective which so fascinated the contemporaries of Brunelleschi. To stipulate, however, that all shapes found within a given sector of the universe are uniformly distorted, hence equally important, and this in accordance with a "law" linked in its workings to a more or less random selection of a point of site (chosen, at best, in accordance with the dictates of "good taste")–this, I say, is to clip the wings of the modern artist too severely for him not to rebel. Such a rule completely ignores the factor of preference, of values assigned on a moral basis. To the artist seeking to impart his personal vision of the world, the first law, therefore, must be to liberate himself from the straitjacket of fixation in space. Not only his eye, his imagination no less than his body, imperiously demands the right to roam, to explore, investigate, choose, obliterate the non-essential, to underscore, magnify – briefly, to re-create his own world:

> To grasp this sorry Scheme of Things entire
> Would not we shatter it to bits–and then
> Remould it nearer to the Heart's Desire!

This much of hostility toward school perspective Cubists and Expressionists have in common. Of the two, the cubist movement was the more intellectually formulated, constituting in its purist days more of a system. Expressionism, never so clearly defined, owns a more visionary background. Lyonel Feininger's painting belongs to neither camp nor school. That some (not all) of his work shows Cubist tendencies is evident; those most familiar with his life know that these qualities were intuitively conceived and not based on adherence to an accepted pattern. The main difference between the Cubists and Lyonel Feininger, constituting an unbridgeable gap, lies in the latter's absolute need for the freest field for the unfolding of fantasy. Never in his life would he have consented to forsake this for no matter how powerful a program of purely formal researches. To the contrary: once the constrictions of fixed space location were removed, he found great value in adapting separate aspects of perspective to his artistic purposes. Distortion could become freely expressive; shapes could be magnified and diminished, vanishing lines could become dynamic thrusts, and through selection, geographical space could be transmuted into imaginative or poetic space. Indeed, the artist's world of the years 1909, 1910, 1911, is quite unthinkable without the visual means of this "liberated perspective," his personal and inimitable way of seeing.

As the illustration "The Disparagers" shows, his system may properly be termed "anti-perspective." The treatment of detail is sufficiently clear and minute to invite close inspection of shapes. To do so is to fall into the trap. In trying to decipher the features of the disparagers we have crossed a threshold and have entered a realm in which the rules whereby we orient ourselves in space are suspended. The single point of site has become a multiple one. The horizon line has been artfully hidden by what looks at first like a "possible" structure, i.e. the viaduct. Accepting this in good faith, we are led to believe that we are looking down into a steep valley, into which the cobblestone street is leading us, and from out of which a group of figures is ascending. The space relation of the tall gentleman swinging his cane to the small man visible between his legs is, in detail, perfectly "possible" if we imagine that we are lying on the ground with our eyes just a few inches above it. A look to the right destroys this comforting possibility. The dimensions of the fat fellow blowing his tin trumpet indignantly at the tall man make it uncomfortably clear that there are giants about. Or dwarfs. We cast an anxious look at familiar objects, such as houses, to gain a clue as to which of the two dimensions is distorted, but here the eye meets the viaduct, and the hope of orienting ourselves in this odd town is shattered for good: this viaduct with its railroad is leading us not to any land we would recognize. According to our original assumption we should have been lying flat on the pavement. If so, the angle of tilt of the viaduct should indicate that its left end is nearer to us, and that it vanishes toward the right. The inside view of its arches belies this: it quite obviously goes off to the left. That being so, we should be located well above the level of the railroad tracks–at least, so perspective has taught us. But not so: we do not even catch a glimpse of them. There was a time when we thought we were looking down into a valley: now we really have to ask: where is the other side of it? A valley has a bottom to it; what is beyond? We look–and only the sky presents itself. There is no other side; we have reached a limit. Perhaps *the* Limit: The Edge of the World. Only the towering bridge seems bravely to promise to take us somewhere, and in a steam train at that; but few of us would volunteer for such a trip. But as a matter of fact we already are on the trip. The artist has lured us into his looking-glass world, and our reliance on that trustiest of space-describing devices, perspective, has proved our undoing.

The awesome and monitory quality of space deprived of the reassuring element of a foothold–which in perspective is given through the relation of groundline to horizonline–is beautifully used in Edgar Allan Poe's "The Sphinx." In this tale the narrator, his mind preyed upon by premonitions of doom, beholds at closest range, a tiny insect crossing his field of vision. His eyes had been examining a distant range of hills and, without his knowledge, had suddenly focused on the "sphinx" descending not, as the narrator thought, a distant hillside but a spiderweb thread an inch from his eye. The description of the insect which follows, is taken from a contemporary work on entomology, and forms as it were an echo to a preceding and horror-struck description in similar terms but on a gigantic scale. The scientific exactitude of the passage in the book, read aloud by his friend, has the effect of restoring the space-reference between subject and object. Retroactively, while reassuring the troubled mind of the beholder of the vision, it enhances the nightmarish quality of the original apparition. What if it *had* been true! The poet has thus created a double "space": the immensity of the relief he experiences at having his vision unravelled for him underlines the depth of his previous despair.

I have dwelt a little longer on this single drawing because it introduces the artistic use of distortion of space in particularly clear terms. Distortion of shapes, which gradually became more and more significant in Feininger's *œuvre,* may be illustrated by another design of later origin: the "Viaduct" of 1919. Superficially speaking, the subject-matter of this woodcut is similar to the "Disparagers." It brings out a point, however, which was not clearly marked in the earlier composition, but which becomes more characteristic as time goes on. It was first revealed to me in the exhibition of 1963 "The Intimate World of Lyonel Feininger." I do not believe it has been made before. The point I wish to bring out is this, that what is usually thought of as the general predilection of the painter for grotesque disregard of natural proportion is actually not general, but rather special. It has been said by many critics that Feininger's towns are peopled by monstrosities swarming or skulking through streets composed of houses they could not possibly enter. Very true: but nobody has yet seen a railway train or a ship depicted by the artist, manned by so disproportionate a crew. Dürer has said that "Man is the measure of all things." Feininger denies this where towns, houses, churches, bridges, windmills, and towers–briefly, where architecture is concerned; but he seems to admit it, and certainly applies the principle of it, in relation to machines: railroad trains, ships, bicycles.
Architectural structures in his paintings are endowed with autonomous life. The church in the pen-drawing "The City at the Edge of the World" is not the only building he has depicted as merrily ready to swallow shepherd and flock! The relative proportions of houses and people undergo significant modifications under his hand: sometimes the buildings, sometimes the populace, seem to gain the

Feininger   The Disparagers   Sunday, July 16th, 1911

upper hand; but a harmonious relation between man and the object made by his brain and hand exists, in his *œuvre*, only in regard to railroads and ships.

Having made this observation and tested its applicability, I reached the hypothetical conclusion that his trains and vessels have the function of being ordering and measuring devices in a mutinous world. Could it be, I asked myself, that they represent specifically male concerns, preoccupied, as such institutions should be, with functioning? If so—if we even speculatively enter into this "train of thought"— we are bound to see in the opposing camp of *architectura*, with Mother *ecclesia* in the van, as its gender implies, the world of woman.

No conscious intention is implied, on the part of the artist, by these speculations. I have gone into them at this stage to draw attention to the use our artist makes of his keen sense of natural proportion, in the breach as well as in the observance. Armed with this key of understanding we are now ready to approach the subject of the toys as they relate to the painted work.

By 1913, the time when he first became interested in toys on a larger scale, he had ceased to be active as an illustrator and caricaturist for something like six years. The life he had led after ending his contract with the Chicago Sunday Tribune had been devoted to developing his pictorial language. It had been a time of intense effort, of fascination with the discovery of a new Self; it had also been a time of private flowering—a very happy time—but, as is perhaps inevitable when a really new work is being prepared and launched, a period without producing an echo in society. We shall see what formal aspects of his caricaturing and painting have contributed to the shaping of his toys and also what light the toys may shed on his other works; but the moral climate out of which that first project of the toy trains evolved seems likewise worthy of mention. My father had been accustomed to success. He had been much sought after as an illustrator; and if there had been much to repel him in his ties with journalism, it is certain, on the other hand, that he had enjoyed the power and the earnings of the prominent cartoonist. In the passages from his letters which follow, a hope to reach a broad public is evident. It was not his primary motif to make a fortune, but it is idle to deny that the idea of being paid for one's labors after years of pure idealism, and the hope of liberating himself from incurring too great a debt of gratitude toward those who had been financially supporting his pioneering toils, had their great appeal.

From his early life on Lyonel Feininger had been fascinated by railroads. They ranked highly amongst the many leanings evinced by the boy "Leo" of which his father had strenuously disapproved. Together

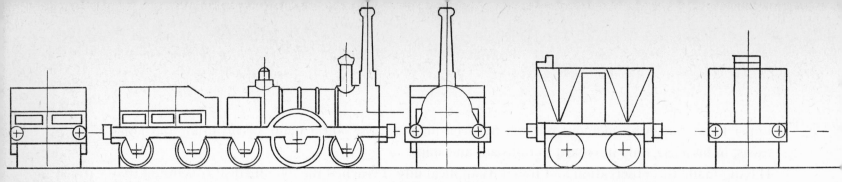

with his boyhood friend Frank K. he had played in a kingdom or republic of the imagination with an elaborate network of railways. In later life, the souvenirs of American railroading were strong. Among the stories of a boyhood in and around New York City which I never tired of hearing was his description of Grand Central Terminal before it was put underground. The essence of many sights must have been contained in the memory of a particularly fine engine–or was it only a particularly fine morning?– on the tracks, half in sunlight and half in shade, beginning to move slowly into the gloom of the over-pass and the last sight of "the rear truck of the tender, the spoked wheels twinkling in the sun." This would have been an engine of the old native type, the "American" or 4-4-0 type. I also heard of the advent of the first "Atlantics" or 4-4-2 types. Rated obsolete long before steam engines had begun to make way for Diesels, they were, in the 1880s, the last word of power and progress. Again my father summed up in an expressive phrase the characteristic aspect of the novelty: the "scissor motion" of the main rod acting on the rear pair of driving wheels, whence the side rod extended to the forward pair. He was very alive to such details. It is true that in the toy engines the running gear was not shown. There was a sound artistic reason for it. Painted main and side rods, valve gear, etc., would have been an anomaly on a system of wheels thought of as rolling when the trains were being moved. For the same reason, only the rims, no spokes, were the décor for the painted wheels of the toys. But it is time to enter into a more precise history of the toy trains.

It must have been in 1911 that my parents became acquainted, in Paris, with Mr. Karl Loewenstein, who saw and admired some toy engines and cars made for the use and enjoyment of the oldest son of Lyonel and Julie Feininger, the author of the photographs in this book and then about four years old. Before long, Mr. Loewenstein had conceived the plan of suggesting to his father, Otto Loewenstein, who owned a factory for wooden toys in Munich, that he interests himself in the possibility of adapting these designs for mass production. By April of 1913 this plan had ripened sufficiently to become a topic of frequent occurrence in my father's letters to my mother, written at Weimar where he was spending the spring and early summer (as he did again in 1914), sketching and painting in self-imposed solitude. Without this separation, we would not have the benefit of following the development in the artist's own vigorous language:

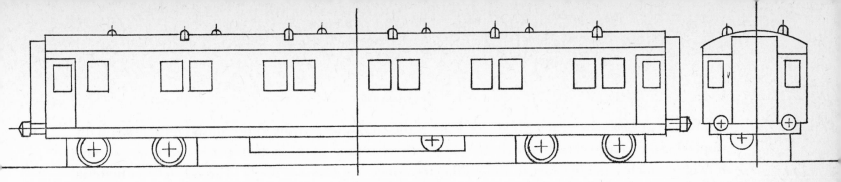

"Do you want to know what made me most hopeful? The fact that obviously the trains were judged most favorably (Heaven forbid that I should permit false hopes to rise!), therefore are representing something new. I shall design contemporary and old types. I even intend to make some ancient, ancient trains of the 1830s . . . To be able to earn money again with my art, and without having to prostitute it at that, will make me ten years younger . . . And the trains will have proper labels; they are going to have the names of the old Railway Companies on them–why? this is one of the main selling points! The oldtimers will have the year of origin, and names, like 'Rocket,' 'Lady of the Lake,' 'John Bull' etc."

(April 7, 1913)

A good deal of correspondence was going on between the manufacturer and my father, centering on technical details of production and on proper legal protection of the invention, terminating in the obtaining of a grant of patent on the strength of the novelty of the "gliding block" (Gleitklotz) of the toys, a wooden block representing the wheel base of each vehicle, upon the sides of which the wheels were painted. During these preliminaries which consumed about a year, he was not idle in carrying the designs further.

"I am thoroughly involved with the models. I am making the trickiest designs, carefully thought out in every detail. Today I ordered buffers at the woodturner's; from now on I shall also have him make steam domes, smokestacks and boilers. It will not be very expensive and infinitely better-looking! One hundred buffers, for a start, will come to slightly more than 1 Mark, and the manufacturer will get a vastly better impression if things are done properly. This work–with a practical purpose besides!– has rejuvenated me into a happy boy of fifteen. The express coaches have turned out beautifully, of much better proportions than before . . ."

(May 26, 1913)

Well before the project became a commercial enterprise, the design problems connected with eventual production engaged his faculties fully. These labors produced such satisfaction that the lack of time for painting is not felt to be a sacrifice.

"Only now it becomes evident how good the trains are, after getting rid of initial mistakes and disproportions. I have ordered more parts from the wood-turner, to be made from very accurate working drawings which I made exact to the millimeter. Since the toys are made of wood, let the material preserve its attractiveness. The lathe develops the wood charm of the various shapes . . ."

(May 27, 1913)

He sounds almost apologetic in describing the pleasure the developing of his ideas is giving him. He reassures himself with the thought of the gains which may be hoped for, because they may feed the family while the pursuit of "modern art" costs money and yields no returns. But the desire to give joy to many, children and adults alike, exists independently and is entirely the same impulse which motivates the painter or the poet.

"I am working at the models from morning till night. The train idea is an inexhaustible source of the most piquant, provoking possibilities. While I am so engaged I feel that I am taking care of our future in a material sense. But I must confess that I am looking for no less than world-wide commercial success. Not just a local 'good idea' for a Christmas present, something that 'will do' for a year or two, but something like the 'Anchor Stone Building Block Sets' or the familiar track sets with their various accessories. I want to start something to gladden and attract every real boy and most grown-ups. I could imagine that adults who like railroads, or did like them when they were children, might buy my models and use them for decoration."

(May 30, 1913)

"I am happy in my model building, for in it I have recovered some of the joys of my youth: invention, construction, let alone the satisfaction with the achievement. I have got a little old English engine now, of the 1830s, with a curved outside frame; this will look absolutely enchanting when I shall have finished painting it."

(May 31, 1913)

The summer months of the year were spent by the entire family in Weimar. The solitude which my father had required in the early season, but which had begun to oppress him, as happened regularly after a spell of intense labors, made way for happy days. They ended, and once again he found himself alone, with the days growing shorter, and with his memories.

"... went out again, in roasting heat ... to the willows at the 'Graben,' halfway to Vollersroda ... shortly before reaching the fence of the Ladies' Horticultural Academy I saw an object by the roadside, made of wood, rectangular, dirty from the rain and covered with earth where it had been trodden on, but still intact: the mail car of Laurence's [my older brother, second son to Lyonel and Julie F.] train which I made for him last Christmas. I picked it up and put it into my pocket. This mute little witness of the one-time presence of our boys moved me strangely!"   (September 14, 1913)

During the fall and winter at Zehlendorf negotiations between himself and Mr. Loewenstein had progressed further. In the spring of 1914 my father, in Weimar again for another season, writes:

"The first few samples of each type (three of each model) give much more trouble than when the tools are going over large quantities. Thank Goodness the models seem to be practicable and easily enough made."   (April 20, 1914)

This refers to trials made experimentally in the Munich factory to test the feasibility of mass production. A certain tenseness becomes perceptible as the moment of decision approaches:

"Yesterday and today I have been all day painting and finishing the samples for L. A lot remains to be done before I can stop tonight, because tomorrow morning they have to be mailed out ... every available surface in the room is covered with toys–I am writing surrounded by paint bowls, dirty brushes, freshly painted trains and an unspeakable odor of Copal varnish. But tomorrow I shall write more. Also, I hope to get some fresh air then. Having to stay indoors all day long in the marvellous weather makes me fidgety. The models have come out very well, now that I can see them in the complete color scheme. I think they will do; of course I am getting impatient to reach a final agreement."   (April 22, 1914)

The transition from the first delights of inspired invention to the tough-minded, prolonged effort of the will which is brought to bear on the project in order to carry it through is highly characteristic.
The contract was settled shortly afterwards. The next letters mention the profits to be expected, which were connected with details of production insisted on by my father and conceded by the

manufacturer. There had been negotiations with another firm, where larger gains were promised, but where the execution of the work was not to the liking of my father. He preferred a good job to larger profits. This was guaranteed by Mr. Loewenstein's "enthusiasm" for the idea, which only "seemed" naïve.

"This project of the railroads is as much an offspring of my brain as any painting and will require understanding care on the part of whomever I entrust it to."   (April 25, 1914)

A few days later he began settling down to the rugged task of starting production:

"I have drawn the conclusions of my having become an inventor, and commercially engaged, in deciding that there can be no thought of painting now–perhaps not for several weeks . . . many points have to be discussed concerning the many unexpected details connected with a proper launching of the enterprise. Design of labels, size and shape of the boxes, number and kind of units per train, etc."
                                                                                          (May 9, 1914)

". . . I love my present labors and am very industrious. Yesterday, Sunday, I worked from seven in the morning until nine-thirty at night, with an hour off for lunch–but it had to be, because the dies for the milling machine had to be designed."   (May 11, 1914)

The intense effort took its toll:

"At last eight sheets of finished working drawings have been mailed off . . . I have a burning cold, which is no help when you have to sit peering over a drawing board, pricking off distances true to the half-millimeter, establishing centers with mathematical accuracy, for if it is not exact the whole thing falls apart! – And yet there is the happy undercurrent of a consciousness that I am engaged in a work which will soon become visible and will gladden hundreds of thousands–something different from 'wretched oil paintings'! – I shan't write more today, I must dash off to find some quinine tablets somewhere. Tomorrow I start on new types, every three to four days L. needs a set of new designs, if the toys are to be on the market by the end of June."   (May 12, 1914)

The trains were made of hardwood, all separate parts being prefabricated by machinery but assembled and painted by hand. As is evident from the letter extracts, the entire procedure was thought out and prepared by my father. Each piece had its proper set of templates, for stencilling on of windows, wheels, and other décor. The entire process of adapting a creatively conceived object for industrial production anticipates quite remarkably by a decade or so the course the Bauhaus was later to follow.

With vivid pleasure I recall the beauty of these trains from the days long gone by – shapes no less than the glorious colors which I love to enumerate: orange and brown, dark red and burnt umber; the many different greens: deep moss-green, cobalt-green, delicate shades of grey-green, of olive in various tonalities, of apple-green; the window patterns: sometimes black, but sometimes in bright hues, light blue or emerald-green (on canary-yellow, a coach which I still have today); the roofs of passenger cars with double rows of staggered little ventilators: brown, oxblood, dark midnight-blue or, as a charming contrast, white. I have a racy express train engine (a "Pacific" or 4-6-2 type) which is all white, with vermilion wheel rims and brown cab windows. The characteristic shapes and proportions of all the rolling stock carried even the most unusual color schemes well. With equal pleasure I remember the beauty, and even the tart and crisp wood smell of a new lot of unpainted trains, recently arrived from the factory. I cannot say at this date whether the enamel colors used for the toy railroad were non-toxic or not. It is possible that the necessity for such precautions had not been perceived in those innocent times. But I cannot help regretting those imaginative and delicate shades of colors. How weary the eye becomes, in our time, of the everlastingly repeated six primary colors of contemporary play equipment, no matter how ingeniously conceived and sturdily as well as safely manufactured!

How far everybody was from seeing any threat in the, to us, sinister time of the late spring of nineteen-fourteen is shown by the fact that Mr. Loewenstein wanted to develop a line of famous French train models for the French market. My father wrote home urgently, requesting my mother to dig through his stacks of railway magazines for illustrations of such material. "Short notice!" he exclaimed. But it got done. By mid-June, the manufactured samples arrived in Weimar for color treatment. He was highly satisfied with the appearance of the French locomotives. He wrote of his certainty that they constituted a valid artistic creation.

And speaking of artistic production, the care lavished on the toy trains had the happiest effect in the studio:

"This activity is very good for me, because I am forced to sustain a mental effort. And–oh wonder!–in between times I am working every day for a few hours at a new painting; rarely yet I have experienced such an unfolding of new feeling for form and color. The interruption of my painting, which I accept not unwillingly but gladly, because of my love of constructing things from childhood on, produces a state of mind in which harmony and reflectiveness become possible. I am very happy and can hardly overstate my gratitude and joy at this enrichment of my days due to the consistent and sustained concentration on the toys. My cold is gone! I enjoy smoking again, there is no coughing! Three cheers for the quinine! And after a three-day rain, at last the skies are clearing somewhat and the world is veiled in a silvery haze. The finches come tripping into my room with grateful steps; soaked and shivering they are as they peck away at their little dishes. Good Heavens how they look after this drenching! quite black, and bristling with wet." (May 14, 1914)

As the sands were running out, the project began to pay off. Already the inventor had been able to write home:

". . . received payment from L. *I* now am sending *you* 320 Marks." (May 16, 1914)

The closeness of the race between his commercial venture and the coming of the collapse of the pre-war world is shown by the dates of the last letters containing news of the undertaking. On June 27th he writes "with his pad on his knees":

"I have not a square inch free on either table or chairs; all is taken up by toys ... the varnish is slow to dry ..." And two days after:

"I have put things in order; now my spirit can move about freely without fear of making dreadful discoveries. All that is left to do is, to finish the labels for the trains, and then a load will be off my chest. – In the evening: The load is gone, labels are done, I am rushing off to the Post Office with them. I am as hungry as a bear, and I am going to treat myself to a glass of wine tonight. – Now I am sitting in the 'Fuerstenkeller' and I've had my 'roastbeefsteak' and am having a second glass of wine. The place is filled with gay and mostly young people, including a few pretty girls–I am at peace, inwardly, artistically, since I have scraped my palette clean and turned all canvases face to wall; I am not worrying about creating any more masterpieces this summer ..."   (June 29, 1914)

On August the first, war was declared and the industries of Europe had to think about producing other things than hardwood toy trains. Nor was the entire project, so hopefully begun and ardently carried forward, ever revived again. Mr. Otto Loewenstein died in the late 20s. Upon the settling of his estate a last box full of trains arrived at my parents' house in Dessau. They finally and belatedly reached their destination in being turned over to the Police and Firemens' Christmas toy collection, making at least a few of the "thousands of children" happy, of whom my father had dreamed in those carefree days that could never return!

With the beginning of the war, the flux and reflux of his relations with society, which had just brought the artist out of his privacy into the business world, the world of manufacturing, now floated him back into a new period of seclusion, more bitter than the first. If his art matured into mastery during these years, morally it was a period of suffering. Compared with his hatred of the war and of the causes which had led to its outbreak, the slow starvation and other privations he had to endure (chief among which was the restriction of his personal liberty due to his having become an enemy alien) were the lesser evils. He could not be under any illusions as to the likely outcome of the struggle. His sympathy with the nation whose guest he had been for so long a time found expression in a letter written in early August, 1915:

"Poor Germany! progressing from victory to victory to her own perdition!"

His Americanism began to appear in a new light. Prior to the war, he had rather enjoyed the flavor of exotic strangeness this background, very visible in his appearance, seemed to have for the natives. Apart from his stature, tall, thin, and angular, accentuated by the long stride in which he took a certain pride, and by his mode of dressing, his clean-shaven visage gave him away amongst a people abundantly addicted to whiskers and mustaches à la Wilhelm II. He became uncomfortably aware of being more conspicuous than suited him. The inward discomfort more than matched the external inconvenience. With increasing speculation about the likelihood of the United States entering the war, his consolation in being a "neutral" dwindled. The conflict of conscience was intensified by the difficulty of owing an allegiance to either side. It was impossible to live in Germany and to refuse a degree of sympathy and admiration for the self-sacrificing attitude of the people. Of the seamy side of the military successes he remained of necessity unaware until after the armistice. To one of his innate pessimism there could be no victors, only losers, in such a contest. His studio became his refuge more than ever before.

Just as he was never able to reconcile for any length of time his need for privacy with his dread of loneliness, so it was with the need for communicating and the fear of giving himself away. There was much to say–the world was full of riches–joy was a possibility, it existed–but there was also another power. It was of a dark nature, not to be denied; it followed one like a friend, but, if resisted, it was ready to turn against one like an enemy. It might wear the aspect of the long-familiar, and again it might take the shape of an unexpected confrontation. Its essence was fantasy, but danger threatened when it assumed reality. The proper form for exorcising it seemed to be the grotesque.

The adoption of the mask need not lessen the faculty of sensation. The search for clear and strong form is the outcome of the felt need to contain the hidden meaning of existence. When found, it is clung to like the precious possession it is. At other times, the lure of the unseen is almost too strong: the clear edges, the ruled lines, begin to waver and to dissolve, and through the rent fabric of design, nocturnal glimpses of another world appear.

Letter extracts and descriptions of toys to follow have the purpose of exemplifying the dual quality of his outlook: monumentality and caprice; clarity and "magic"; revelation and disguise. – As we last saw the artist, he was about to disappear into his studio, whence he will emerge at the proper time with the big exhibition at the "Sturm" in 1917. We may begin our survey of formal and emotional elements of the art which will be shown there with a retrospective declaration of early intentions:

"When I started, back in 1907, my first painting, I was but a caricaturist and my intentions regarding oil painting were vague. My only outlet seemed to be the poster. Or, to put it a bit more exactly, my ideal was, to build up pictures formed of silhouetted objects. Like some of M.'s [my mother's] early paper cut-outs. And again, I had seen *Schiessbuden* [shooting gallery] figures, cut of sheet iron and painted in a simple array of more or less violent colors, with no modelling. . . Light and shade and all the atmosphere you can impart to a painting will still not solve the ultimate problem of painting, which is based upon spatial interrelationships– and in modern painting, which in many ways is less 'modern' than 13th and 14th century art, it is the disposition of the spatial structure which is important above all the other elements of the picture, and this spatial structure must be logically reduced to the greatest possible simplicity of parts. Simple, large color planes keyed together on the painting surface, is the aim; not photographically diversified modulation of color. Clear forms, which carry the space element and the subject in all simplicity and directness–that, in a new way, is what makes Turner's art so great and lasting . . ."   (July 2, 1946)

We see here Lyonel Feininger discussing, in terms of design, the problem of space which Paul Klee had approached from the angle of cosmic kinship. In this choice, I see strong evidence of a preference. It is the male side that speaks, an expression of the *will*. The other, the darkly fantastic, "cosmic" and intuitive and female side is voiced through many encounters with "nature," of which I have chosen, as an introductory offering, some meetings with *birds*.

Like many people, he was very fond of them. In Weimar, that town of large gardens, parks, and orchards, a rich bird fauna came to his window sill, where with loving care he kept a supply of various tempting foods. His letters home abound in little sketches of the constant coming and going of his feathered guests, with enumeration of species, accounts of their behavior, comparisons of temperament, etc. But some of these ornithological adventures seem to me to differ from ordinary bird-watching. Not only the description of the event, but the reaction of the artist, seem to me worthy of attention:

"Yesterday I came to a village half-way up the Ettersberg; besides picturesque houses and steep lanes I saw, toward the end, a marvellous, beautiful bird–a peacock! Perched on top of a gateway, exactly in the middle, the creature was exhibiting itself. I felt something like awe, to see the electric-blue of its neck, the most magnificent intense blue-green imaginable–to me, this was a mystical animal. I made several attempts to draw it. Finally I whistled to it, whereupon it emitted a sound which almost knocked me over with fright: something like a horrendous burst trumpet of doom! – This, to come from the tiny, delicate head at the end of the conical, erect, metallic-blue neck! – After this note, the marvellous beast flew down to the dirty pavement, balancing its five-foot tail behind it–I have never seen anything to equal it in perverse beauty. I was in love with every movement. Nearby two geese were cackling and hissing like hideous and evil old women. And the peacock paid no attention, it walked this way and that, bending and turning, the neck like a fabulous serpent with the most improbable curvings and twistings–and always that little head with white cheeks and black markings, fiercely blue on top and so tiny! completely mystical! Try to visualize this bird at the last, when it had posted itself in a corner of masonry upon a piece of mossy ground–the green of the tail against the moss-green, the blue against the stone-color of the wall!–and its yellow legs! – Finally a peasant and his wife arrived and called the bird by name: 'Hans!' and unlocked the gate, and it walked through and was gone . . ."   (May 4, 1913)

On the other side of the Atlantic, forty years later, another vision was engendered through the agency of a bird:

". . . a strange-appearing, black and rusty grey and white gull–if it was indeed a gull–was first seen swimming steadily out, against contrary wavelets (on Thursday, which was fresh and brilliantly blue)

Lyonel Feininger
in his studio
in New York, 1951

Lyonel, T. Lux and Tomas Feininger
at the Central Park Model Yacht Pond, New York, 1951

and, without swerving, without peering for nourishment, seemingly only for the experience of paddling sturdily straight 'out to sea,' this truly strange creature swam–rather weakly, it seemed to us–against these lapping waves which almost covered its breast; and the next day we saw it again, it lay quite recumbent and with spread, drooping, white-edged black wings, on the low-tide pebbles and disorder, with its head bent down over its breast, paying no attention to anything at all, simply dying. Somehow it had returned from its argosy of the day before, to the same deserted bit of shore, and with closed eyes was waiting for its end. I tried to sketch it, but it lay in such disorder . . . that I could not make a clear sketch . . . it had a strangely shaped bill–not a spoon bill. . . Well, my impression is that it had one last feeble swim out into the open, before giving up the struggle of bird-existence. We have looked for it every day since, but it is gone . . ."

(September 12, 1953)

It seems to have struck the writer of these observations as specially worth noting, in both cases, that birds come to the ground, or that they are brought down. And is it an undue fancy to see in the comparison of the pea-fowl from Malaya and the Thuringian geese, a likeness of "the American" striding long-leggedly through a race of squat and earthy gnomes?

In later life, the ground and things appearing on it, became more and more attractive to him. In his last years he amused himself with making intimate camera studies of tiny areas of the earth at his feet: flowers, fallen leaves, minute weeds, gravel, sand. He loved to study these color transparencies, greatly enlarged, of an evening in slide projection. As a young painter he had already made pictorial use of patterns of street pavement, textures of cobblestones. This man of aerial visions seems to have felt a need for keeping a firm hold on the ground.

The life and destinies of trees moved him quite apart from their function in landscape. The designer in him preferred them bare of leaves, gaunt and silhouetted, mere accents on the land; but he loved to observe the rhythm of vegetal life and the cycle of the seasons, preferring or rejecting none. In a letter written from Stockbridge, Massachusetts, he describes how it took several men a week to

"bring low one of Nature's magnificent growths, a tree centuries old... until finally nothing but a tortured, truncated monument stands denuded of its recent glory, reaching pitifully up to Heaven

45

in its dying agony. But two weeks ago this giant was an outstanding glory, clothed in red and gold foliage."

One cannot tell whether there is any conscious intention of analogy of this description with the remark on the next page of the letter:

"I believe I may have mentioned . . . that, as the weeks pass by, the size of my output in drawings decreaseth? . . . I wonder whether I shall really get to oil painting again?"   (October 29, 1954)

On the other hand, in the passage below there is a considerable degree of awareness of his own reactions, as well as a grateful acceptance of something which exists:

". . . outside the Metropolitan Museum a few grand old trees in the late sunlight cast rich shadows over the façade–just delightful. It seems almost queer that I so stress the impressions of trees, and sun, when I do nothing about them in my painting. But their essence is what enters into my happy mood and doubtless helps somewhat to soften my customary severities of style."   (November 1, 1953)

He was very fond of the Christmas season. He loved to have his family and friends around, he eagerly counted the days until the longest night ushered in the return of the light, and he also regularly insisted upon a Christmas tree. In his last years he was content to

"just sit quietly in the evening and look at the little Christmas tree lit up in its corner; it is a very odd little one, quite irregular and fits in very well and disturbs no one . . ."   (December 29, 1954)

One really feels compelled to ask whom it could possibly "disturb"? Is it not as if he were talking, not of a tree, but of an old friend in poor circumstances, perhaps a pensioner being allowed his room and board and a little pocket money?

But the symbol of cyclical return calls up echoes in the author as well as in his subject. With the thought of the old pair sitting and looking at their tree in New York, my mind reverts to earlier holiday seasons, and to my theme. I begin with another quotation at the half-way mark on the road back:

"Christmas and New Years Day are over; . . . we've had a very quiet time of it, with Laurence. . . This year, I gave the use of my 'atelier' . . . for the celebration. We had a very pretty, very irregularly shaped 'Doppeltanne' with a whale of a lot of pine cones on it and trimmed it with all our old Zehlendorf figures I made for you boys when you were little, back in 1915."   (January 9, 1937)

Nineteen-fifteen was the second Christmas of the Big War; Zehlendorf, the suburb of Berlin, then a grass-grown, sleepy old town, now since many years absorbed in the Metropolis. The suburban train connecting with the Capital ran through plowed fields and open farm land, labored over by war prisoners as I well remember: Frenchmen, Russians. . . But the tree ornaments I have before me now, they have survived. They are flat pieces of maple wood, sawed out with a jigsaw and gaily painted and varnished: Sun, Moon and Stars; a Comet; Angels playing, not to say braying, on weirdly contorted instruments; the Miller and his Mill; a Jolly Fellow in a Dutch Sailboat; a Balloon; Children in Pinafores; a Young Lady in High Button Shoes; a Hausfrau with an Apron-full of Gleaned Coals (a wartime sight); a Gruff German Stationmaster with his absurd wand of office, sort of an abstract fly swatter, without the "official" raising of which no train could legally depart in old-time Germany—this is the innocent-looking host occupying the front of the stage. But the festive tree harbored other pieces, casting perhaps a deeper beam of intelligence into the depths of my father's humor. There were some sculptured wooden heads, their four-square, jowly features somewhat surly in character. One or two were painted in simple, abstract colors; another was a bristlingly mustachioed warrior with the helmet of a Uhlan; but the last one was a very definite and positive Devil. Yes—with blue horns. His ivory-black and white features, although somewhat simian, express not so much evil as the sly and wise, cynical disillusionment of the Troll of the Norwegian Folktales. He too is a guest bidden to the feast! Perhaps he was smuggled in through the side door. There is a German colloquialism, used to explain an incomprehensible impulse: "The Devil rode me . . ." Yes, it applies: not intentionally and purposely wicked, not sinister, there was yet something Puck-like and not altogether harmless in my father's humor; we shall see other instances hereafter. Possibly we have here an irruption of "cosmic consciousness," comically expressed. Whether or no, need I say that this little blue-horned head is particularly dear to me?

From the Christmas tree and its ornaments we must shift our vision to the floor below it, where two or three years later a fine batch of toy ships made its appearance. Of this noble fleet–four sailing ships, two steamers and two side-wheelers–only one exists today. I have a very distinct recollection of them all, however, not only of their appearance, but of the extraordinary pleasure they gave. I remember their colors: the square-riggers were white and grey, with black painted ports, Naples-yellow masts and yards, green deck houses; one of the steamers was red and black, the other violet and grey, etc. But of the single survivor I should like to say a little more, for it is one of the small things that incorporate more than meets the eye. Itself the product of remembrance, it now in its turn produces memories.

It is a Hudson River sloop, and belongs to his youth in New York. In the land-locked streets of Zehlendorf, he had evoked a thirty-year-old memory in order to whittle a toy for his boys. A letter gives a hint of the lineage of the souvenir. The vessel referred to in it appears, on the photograph of which he is writing, in the distant background, about the size of a thumb-tack:

"The beautiful photograph of the 'City of Worcester' is thrilling in the way it recalls the scenes of the Eighties at the Battery and on the Hudson; . . . it brings a glow to my heart that you got it for me and sent it . . . there is one of the old-time Hudson River Sloops that I remember so well; you'd see them hugging the New Jersey shore, the most inconspicuous of vessels, lowly, serving the humblest of purposes; . . . the incredibly lofty, raking and lean-appearing rig, the mainsail loose-footed and with the brails crossing it in a series of hanging festoons, a greyish buff color. . . I recall one occasion when the ferry taking me to New Jersey paused before its slip, in order to let one of these sloops creep by, and I was struck by the sight of fresh paint spread on in almost delicate shades of white and pale blue on the sides of the battered hull, and the strip-moldings . . . in a triple row were as carefully picked out in color as if it had been a yacht. And–alas!–the cargo consisted of sacks of dirty and worn appearance containing rags, old bottles and paper scraps. . . It is a satisfaction to me, after all those years, that I, if only this once, had taken thought to examine and appreciate one of them."

(September 12, 1938)

The little toy sloop now before me, sawed out of a piece of firewood forty-six years ago, has its sides painted white and pale blue; they are battered enough, nor is the paint fresh anymore. The "raking and lean" rig consists of four shrouds and two backstays, half of them trailing alongside brokenly. *Voces fidelium!* My memories of this war-time Christmas are already older by seventeen years than the souvenir of the obsolete sloop was when the artist sat down to carve it.

As for the whereabouts of the rest of the fleet, we must assume that the Feininger boys "loved them to pieces": I cannot otherwise account for their disappearance.

*

The period of withdrawal which began at the outbreak of the war ended with the big solo exhibition of my father's at the "Sturm" in 1917. With this event he became a public figure. As the war entered its last year of frenzied madness, the forces which were to be so instrumental in shaping post-war Europe were already active beneath the surface. Overshadowed by the war effort of the doomed nation, as were the slim frames of some of the members of this group by the "field grey" uniform, the artists, poets, and intellectuals of the circle around Herwarth Walden of the "Sturm," were powers of peace. Lyonel Feininger's art had been moving steadily toward his logical and inevitable public appearance and acclaim. Beginning with his now famous participation in the *Ersten Deutschen Herbstsalon* in 1913–at which time Franz Marc, from whose hand the invitation came, could still write that "the only reason you were not asked earlier to join us was, that our circle did not know of your work until Alfred Kubin directed our attention to it"–the eyes of a small group of men, destined to have wide-ranging influence in the future, had been on him. Walter Gropius was one of these. In the spring of 1919, my father was asked, and had decided, to join the school to be founded in Weimar, known afterwards as the Bauhaus.

It would be difficult to overstate the impact of the new direction the life of Lyonel Feininger had taken. Possibly, the telescopic perspective of time makes the many and drastic changes appear more sudden than they were. The ending of the war; the revolution; cessation of the irksome state of "enemy alien" with its attendant police surveillance; the appointment to teach, and to be the head of the Graphics Workshop at the Bauhaus; the move of self and family to Weimar, leaving behind his home of eleven years' habitation–all this was compressed in a space of eighteen months, counting from the time of his emergence, with the exhibition of 1917, as a major figure in contemporary art.

With the Weimar phase of the Bauhaus, he entered into a period of his life which many, myself included,

49

see as the peak of his powers, where all his faculties were brought into play, including some he may not have known he possessed. The exercise of one of them, his newly discovered ability to speak publicly on matters of educational policy, which was necessary for one who had formed part of the original nucleus of the Bauhaus faculty, ran directly opposite to his personal inclination. The role he played in helping to launch the enterprise is well documented and will probably be the subject of future studies. In keeping with my plan, I shall try to outline the moral and intellectual climate in which his creations of this, and subsequent periods, were conceived.

Consider, for example, the variety of human contacts the new position brought into his life. The personality of Gropius may well head the ranks. He was a warm and devoted personal friend, to be sure; but in the official or public relationship with the new director, there were other aspects to be dealt with: great differences of temperament, of opinion, of interpretation of such questions as the goals and the meaning of an art education and its function in a society which had just begun to form.

50

What *was* art anyway? What could its purpose be in the post-war era? What was best for the students? And who were these students? How much should their wishes be considered? "Form," Gropius said; "Expressionism," my father felt. He was almost awed at the indications of new talent amongst the generation which had so recently been freed from military duties and of whose aims and ideals he had been unaware so long as he had counted himself as one of the "new generation." Not the least of the consequences of his sudden transformation was his finding himself belonging to the "previous" generation! There are letters of his in which he expresses doubt as to what one could still hope to teach such talent; before long, however, his perceptions adapted to the standards of post-war aims and longings and he began to see that there was still much to be done. Almost with relief, he noted the signs clearly showing the need for training. What seemed most urgently wanted was to give students time for growth, encouragement; induce them to study nature while keeping the eye on the future need for "overcoming nature" in their creations; but from the first, the Bauhaus and all in it seemed to suffer from lack of time. New points of dissent!

Close and friendly contact with fellow artists of equal rank was a new experience. Friendships were made, based on recognition of, and respect for each other's rights, differences of approach, and educational views. The ties formed between my father and Paul Klee, Wassily Kandinsky, Georg Muche, and Gerhard Marcks endured through all the vicissitudes and changes which were to come to the lives of them all; and through the most turbulent periods of the Bauhaus the feeling of solidarity derived from and given to his fellow artists was a support and a source of strength.

In his relations with students he also found much good. He who had never really had a teacher, found that he could be one. The enthusiasm of his students, their devotion to the future, deeply impressed

him. He was delighted at their gift for improvising feasts and pageants and he participated in these with much pleasure. On their part, the students responded with admiration to his innate democratic outlook which led him to treat them as equals–privately and publicly he disclaimed the title of Professor bestowed on the Bauhaus Masters by the Government–and to the end he had their confidence and support. I well remember the surprise, no more than the beauty and the festive spirit, of a serenade offered to my father under the windows of the house where we lived, a large and silent body of young people suddenly filling the quiet street in the dusk of a summer evening, each holding aloft a glowing paper lantern, startling us boys out of early slumbers. A very moving experience it must have been to my father.

His new duties brought him in contact with less admirable members of society as well. In Weimar as well as later in Dessau, the Bauhaus had to endure much hostility from anti-republican parties. The political climate of Weimar, in particular, was unfavorable to the new school from the beginning. Opposition took, besides the more traditional aspects of refusing to vote funds and moral support, the unlovely forms of slander and calumny. In common with the other masters, my father was frequently called upon to meet with unsympathetic members of the State Legislature, in the hope of convincing them that the school was neither a hotbed of anarchy, nor given over to free love, nor an asylum for the criminally insane. Periodically, the studios and workshops would be open to a sullen host, who responded to Gropius' energetic and clear commentaries on the work in progress, with offensive silence or with malapropos questions. While this resistance, varying from open attacks to underground intrigues, had the effect of confirming and solidifying the loyalty of faculty and students to the common ideal, it is too well known how it achieved its end. Less than seven years from the start, the town of Weimar which had been entered with cheers, was left with groans.

At the outset, of course, the hopeful aspects prevailed. From the revolution of 1918 to approximately 1923–the year of the big Bauhaus Exhibition–my father yielded, perhaps not unwillingly, to an optimism which was really foreign to his nature. For years he had had the longing to be useful to society: here, it seemed, was the place in which to serve.

Of the stimulating and desperate, new and age-old, gay and maddening, ridiculous and pathetic sensations of this period, the toys are the expression. In their nature and in their form, they belong to the irrational part of Lyonel Feininger's world, which the orderly and measured model railroads had tried to regulate.

And had not that reasonable and rational venture of the toy trains been cut off in its budding, scarcely flowering, stage, before any fruit could be harvested, by the supreme irrationality and witch-like fury of the war? Who will say whether a grain of this causality had not filtered into his consciousness? Was not the Italy of Mussolini defended by the argument, advanced by overseas admirers of this régime, that "at least, he had made the trains run on time"? Be that as it may, the post-war world seemed abandoned to a reign of fantasy. Our little figurines are solidified manifestations of it.

If the model trains of 1914 had been reasonable, the toys of the post-war years don't even try to be. Quite the contrary: proportion, harmony of related parts, any possibility of "functioning" in the accepted sense of the word, has been abandoned. After 1914, my father made no more trains; from around 1920 on, houses, people and ships, are the subject-matter of the carved playthings, which have become, to the majority of his public, *the* toys par excellence. These toys have a two-dimensional counterpart in the smaller woodcuts made during the same period (1918 – 1921 approximately), just as the carved figures of the last years have a corresponding graphic development in the pen-and-watercolor designs which we will encounter later.

They are bits, pieces, splinters of Expressionism. And what is that? The mood or the climate whence these manifestations arrive prompts the use of extravagant language. To those who do not shun Expressionist criticism, I should like to recommend a little book which admirably catches the spirit of the work and of the period: "Lyonel Feininger" by Willi Wolfradt (Junge Kunst, Band 47, Leipzig 1924, Verlag von Klinkhardt & Biermann). But I, at the sobering distance of more than forty years, must confine myself to mere hints of what I sense in the term of "Expressionism." It is not the pursuit of Ideal Form, so much is clear. Is it ugly? By whose standards? Perhaps by those of the contemporary post-war society, so richly sprinkled with profiteers, swindlers, conspirers, traitors, assassins, cranks, and maniacs? Is it wicked? Listen to the pot calling the kettle black! What is good? Ask rather: has it arms and legs? Not always, but it does have *life*.

A life of its own; an autonomous life. Its very lawlessness seems to be governed by some kind of non-rule, something anti- or other. One feels that the citizens of the "City at the Edge of the World"– some of them–would be almost ready to think if only their hats would let them.

I can't remember when exactly the toy town had begun; but in 1921 already my father writes that "the time for my periodical craze for making toys for Christmas is approaching. Every year I get the urge to saw wood into bits and paint them in bright colors. The boys take it for granted that I shall make 'mannequins' for them."

(November 19, 1921)

These "boys" were then 15, 12, and 11 years old, respectively. Speaking for my brother Laurence and myself, I may say that we still did "take it for granted" that there would be new citizens for the growing city; but in view of his continuing production year after year one may presume that there was a direct reward for the artist in the gratification of his "annual urge." In 1931 he still wrote of the "usual toy-making season," but soon afterward, his saw and chisel began a long rest, not to be broken until he had entered his old age.

But what, who, were the little "bits of sawed wood"? Who was the model? It began so innocently. The first figures could almost have come from the traditional Silesian home industries: little gentlemen in blue coats, with tidy rows of painted buttons; little ladies with the proper undulatory outlines; neat stick arms glued to the sides, pink faces and hands, etc. But almost at once much greater liberties were taken: the next batch revelled in green or yellow faces, truncated torsos, angular, knobby. If they were limbless, they had hats, as wildly expressive as the overgrowths on heads and pronotums of tropical insects. There were silly German policemen with their incredible spiked helmets, those symbols of Wilhelmian Imperialism of which the decrees of the Weimar Republic had deprived the force; a sailor in yellow oilskins and southwester hat, with a meerschaum pipe as big as an arm (which he did not have); old ladies (of the ex-Grand-Ducal court type) wrapped in shawls and wearing ante-bellum bonnets; a young one, in chrome-orange and cobalt-green, sporting a fine (although wooden) parasol; a flock of black-coated, lemon-visaged gentry with top hats; shapes striding, skulking, perched high on posts or squatting, toadlike, on the ground. An unmistakably "female" figure–the only one I can recall owning a distinct pair of legs–constructed along the lines of the dollar sign ($), was a portrait of the "hired girl," Minna, whose buxom forms were first commemorated in the shape I have described by my sarcastic and teen-age brother Andreas, to my father's uproarious delight.

The appearance of two particular figures in this early group gives a hint of the role which toy-making may have played for the artist. We see a pair of clerics, in whose garb, especially their hats, the traveled connoisseur recognizes the Jesuit without difficulty. In the skeletal leanness of the tall one, the pudgy squatness of his companion (a kind of Father Brown, a character much esteemed by my father), one sees something like the classical music-hall pair of comedians. Middle-aged movie-goers may recall

54

Laurel and Hardy, and old-timers the Danish stars of long ago, Pat and Patachon, as examples taken from the screen, of this kind of polarity. One may ask: why attack the clergy? The answer would be: it is not being attacked; it is only mentioned in this special way, because it belongs in the artist's world. It expresses his divided, problematical attitude toward this portion of humanity, which he had evinced earlier in his caricatures and paintings, where the figure of the "Jesuit" was treated with a gusto speaking of anything but indifference.

I have said that the toy town and its inhabitants have only an early and a late period. The photographs combine examples of both. The long hiatus between the two phases, during which all this fantastic life went underground, remains visually unillustrated. What, in the first attempts, was forecast dimly in the way of silent persiflage and perhaps quite untoy-like thoughts, is brought out triumphantly in the late ones.

In the post-World War II winter whittlings, the artist achieves an absolute climax of the witches' sabbath begun so long ago. The last restraints have been discarded and "spooks," regular ghosts in white winding sheets, even a horned, blue shape, doing their best to look "harmless," make their appearance. There are also, for the first time, animals: owls, cats, an elephant. The New York figurines, recalling some of the mysterious paintings of Piero di Cosimo, may be theriomorphic humans or anthropomorphic animals. Some of the whittled specimens of childhood are highly suspect in this regard. The doubtful view taken by the artist of the contemporary newest generation is reflected also in the pen-and-watercolor drawings of the same period. Formally speaking, the late figures are a little more "impressionistic" than their predecessors. They are less angular, more undulant; edges are effaced, and surfaces more activated by means of applied décor: rows of protuberant buttons, horns, tails, etc. The problematical clergy is not missing from the late cast: they have received promotions. Instead of the former black coats, we see their representatives in crimson and violet robes.

The houses of this weird community are Gothic, broken-backed, cramped and colorful, gable-fronted, with overhanging upper stories, huge chimneys and steep roofs. The church of the village of Gelmeroda, famous for thirteen compositions of large paintings, is enlarged about a hundred times in proportion to the North German cathedral which is the principal house of worship of the town. The two churches are products of different years, probably only a year or two apart. The dimensions of the toys may be of interest: the average figurine is well under three inches high, the tallest edifice little more than a foot high. But these dimensions were shaped by a man who has said more than once that proportion did not depend on inches and that "if you had it in you, you could be monumental on a postage stamp."

In the town, the seasons were somewhat irregular. Snow-covered rooftops towered above rectilinear bits of green lawn on which anglers were squatting. The first set of houses had been elaborately painted. But gradually, as the "children's" expectations lessened, the more sculptural possibilities of the sawed-out toys attracted my father more, as he kept making additions to the "town." A set of house-like forms was designed at last, pure white, painted over the rough surfaces of the sawn and split wood, which had not been sandpapered. This set he made for his own amusement, a present to himself, and he kept regrouping the units in various ways to explore their formal relationships. Someone in the plastic workshop of the Bauhaus made a plaster cast of one of these groups. Both the fact of the moveable units, and the preservation of the wood character in a homogenous material like plaster or bronze, anticipate more recent approaches of contemporary sculptors. The cast house-group, as well as some of the toy caravels of the town, have served as a theme for several picture compositions.

The fun my father had while making the early toys is not documented in his own words, so far as I know. Of the works of the late period, as we shall see in some detail later on, the watercolor grotesques are occasionally mentioned in his letters. Here it is interesting to note that he confines himself to statements relating to their formal interest. He avoids almost studiously any reference to their visionary content and meaning. He may not have felt a comparable need of accounting for the carved figures, since they were "only toys"; at least, he never writes of them. But in their provoking, restless inquisitiveness, their air of bursting with answers to last questions which they would divulge if only someone would ask them, carvings and drawings are alike, chips off the same block.

The word "harmless" has been used by writers in describing Lyonel Feininger's fantasies. I agree with this term only as far as conscious intention goes. The underlying content or intimation of some of the expressions of humor and *diablerie* is another matter. Nor do I have in mind anything like a deprecatory interpretation of a nightmare, a rationalizing attitude, but something more akin–in purpose–to counter-magic. If the last of the carved figurines seem to be exploding with merriment, some of the very early fantastic visions are darkly harboring hidden knowledge. The pen drawing of the "Excursion Train" has this premonitory quality.

As an evocation of old times–the infancy of railroading–it seems to invite one "harmlessly" to join this illustrious group, so full of measured and decorous dignity, calmly permitting its Biedermeier worthiness to lend splendor to the festive occasion. Ladies and gentlemen are embarking on their "Pfingst-Ausflug," the traditional German excursion into the country on the holiday of the Pentecost. The period, we should judge from the costumes and details of the train, is the early 1830s.

For an account of a train ride of a holiday crowd of select citizens in 1831, I should like to quote from a favorite book of my father's, lying at my elbow as I write. A span of forty-five years is covered by inscriptions on the fly-leaf in his handwriting, the first being: "Xmas 1909," the last: "read May 5th, 1954."

"Opening of the Albany & Schenectady Railroad. September 24, 1831 . . . we proceeded in carriages . . . to the starting place of the railroad, about two miles from the city . . . When the engine was getting up steam, passengers were crowding into the cars . . . David Matthew, the engineer, dropped oil on the frictional surfaces . . . then mounted on the unprotected footplate, ready to start. John T. Clark, who was the first conductor, mounted to the seat at the back of the tender, tooted upon a tin horn, and this famous cavalcade started. So did the horses belonging to a concourse of farmers . . . with their wives, families, cousins and aunts . . . when the engine gave forth the first exhaust, the horses started away in frightful terror . . . The passengers . . . had their own share of excitement . . . the loose couplings

jerked the train so violently that the people were thrown into confused heaps ... There was no spark arrester, so the force of the exhaust threw out a volume of black smoke, freely mixed with sparks, coal, cinders and lumps of half-burned pine. The sparks found their way into the eyes and ears of the passengers, down their necks and into every crevice of their clothing. Those who carried umbrellas raised them to ward off the fiery downpour; but they soon took fire, and the train held a frantic crowd who slapped out the flames, destroying their own and their neighbors' garments. People by the wayside supposed that the train was carrying a load of maniacs."

(Angus Sinclair: "The Development of the Locomotive Engine", New York, 1907)

It is very difficult for me not to believe that my father had this strangely anti-Pentecostal descent of "fiery tongues" from above in mind when he allowed his stately party to approach the iron monster belching blackness so unconcernedly. The touching faith of mankind in the efficacy of its own creations, while admirable, is nevertheless hybrid and, as such, needs to be castigated. If the artist does this *ridendo*, he keeps the laugh to himself, confident that "time will tell."

Another pen-and-ink drawing of the early days conveys its message in a more abstract language ("Women in an Exhibition," 1908). Of course one could confine one's attention to formal matters: the handling of space or, as my father called it, the "keying together" of positive and negative volumes, the design of white, hatched, grey wash and black areas, carefully brought into pictorial relationship to the picture edges. But such a study would be missing the best part of the "exhibition," the content, the satirical wit of the social criticism: what is it that the ladies are contemplating so meditatively, all except the central figure? She, sparsely elegant in gently angular lines, is held in space by a spectral, bosomy shape formed in part by the back of her head. It is as if she had left the purely feminine attributes behind her. She alone, by not exhibiting the charms which are holding her sex-mates spellbound, is in a position to establish a rapport with the pictures on the wall. The others remain narcistically uninvolved, absorbed, remote. The drawing is a clear statement of the confrontation of opposing forces, a theme which remained dear to the artist up to the late period. Toward the end, however, the theme received the modification of one of the opposing parties becoming more and more subjective (the spectator or the recording artist) while the apparitions constituting the other side assumed an often quite terrifying objectivity.

I repeat that it does not matter whether the artist is fully, partly or not at all aware of what can be read between the lines, so long as through the agency of his sensitive perceptions and his skilful hand, the message he has received is put down. Monitory attitudes become premonitions: as the consciousness of an artist's public is growing, additional meanings can and will be discovered in works deriving from intuitive and inspirational sources. I am thinking of Goya's "Disparates," Paul Klee's work in general, Lyonel Feininger's late, tiny scribblings. Form, at its purest, is by definition an expression of an Idea; it is thus impossible to conceive of soulless "form." But if, then, the soul necessarily dwells in form, the possibility of the form's communicating with him who beholds, exists. Intelligibility, interpretation of the message, correct decoding of the cryptogram—these are questions of degree only.

The following section is a study of the workings of an artist's mind in regard to his art. The aim is, to illustrate in the painter's own words wherever possible, the interweaving of two forces: the products of memory and of longing for distant times, places and experiences, and, in keen contrast thereto, his determination to handle form, to bend it to his will, apparently almost regardless of content. We shall see both a response to, and a rejection of new scenes; and we shall see that they are really old ones, disguised. Between the poles of yearning to reconstruct old times and his premonitions of things to come, what happens to the Here and Now? In regard to this question, his old age in New York is very enlightening, because in those years he achieved a gradual conquest of that passing moment at which futurity is transformed into historical antiquity. I view this result, which is intimately connected with his return to his native city, as the triumph of his life. For this reason I propose to document it with letter extracts at some length.

In this study of the background of his visions, chronology reveals its subjection to the theory of relativity. Considerations of preference, of personal values, of moods, prevail throughout, over the relative unimportance of accidental location or of age. The best guide, therefore, is the subject-matter of the works to be discussed, and the various invisible threads connecting it to other, identifiable themes. Lyonel Feininger's love for figure compositions had never been entirely dormant. The period of least activity in this field would be from the mid-twenties to the end of the thirties. During the Second World War figurative motifs reappear. At first derived from old nature sketches or "notes" (as he called them), they soon became translations of the life around and within him, here and there seasoned by identifiable flashbacks into his personal past.

Again I should like to direct attention to the emphasis the artist gives to the formal interest of his creations. Careful to avoid the appearance of over-valuing their importance, he says that he has been working at

". . . very trivial things; let us say: for practice–because the formal treatment of these grotesque distortions serves me when I turn my hand to more weighty compositions; and also, because I enjoy harking back to drolleries . . . somehow, the little doodlings seem to me, at least on formal grounds, to outrank the more exacting large-scale watercolors."   (November 5, 1954)

This sounds as if he were playing while drawing these little groups. A note of apology is perceptible: pleasure alone is not enough to justify a work by the master. But there is another appeal besides the formal one:

"It is good not to let everything disappear that we find fun in doing. Too much slips away from us as it is. And what pleasure it gives to the one who receives these skittish manifestations. To me, half the reward is in sending away one *in lieu of a letter* [the italics are mine], and thus avoiding too strenuous a task, such as writing of unmentionable thoughts, which too often manage to sneak into writing, and which are not always very interesting."   (December 5, 1954)

The minimizing, deprecatory note can be sensed. Be the purport of the "messages" what it will, two things are clear (besides the hints given by certain references to subject-matter): the message is first "received" by the artist, then passed on to a friend. The other is, that if the artist was not always very clear as to what the message was saying, he knew very well what he did *not* want to say: "unmentionable thoughts," surely dealing somehow with age, with a process of summing up the findings of a long life; reactions to the shrinking of physical powers, mute protests against the irritations of daily life; the whole–philosophy and flea-bites–constituting a look backward and, perhaps, a look ahead as well; a series of glimpses of what Joseph Conrad has called (in the "Mirror of the Sea") "the landfall and departure blending in one" of the Last Voyage.

Speaking of this manner of communication we find, that to the list of terms descriptive of the artist's approach to subject-matter, we must add another: circumscription. This may stand for the indirect approach, for the handling of a theme which one can neither talk about freely, nor yet dismiss from one's mind. If, visually speaking, this procedure employs a set of personal signs and symbols, the manner in which it is conveyed resembles the "MS in a bottle." Lyonel Feininger is one of the few people who never kept a journal, however privately; but the little figure fantasies (there must be several hundreds of them) come close to a diary kept in a secret language. And was there ever a diary written without the subliminal hope that somewhere, someone would understand?

From another letter which begins by tracing out a grey mood, we learn something a little more distinct not only about the identity of some of the figures in the drawings, but also about their emotional value for their maker:

"Late afternoon on Columbus Day. A pale, featureless fall day; vapors, not really clouds, formless and colorless, pass overhead and merge into the scarcely defined horizon. A rainy day would depress me less than the poor faltering light filtering through straggly gaps in the murk; and a chill air which cannot quite become a breeze to clear the murk . . . I packed up my drawing materials this morning, my suitcase is closed and I have not now the resource–the never-failing one–of making a few crazy little ghosties on paper and putting bright colors on the lines. All the long evenings I have been creating demons, pixies, 'Mysterious Petes,' and lantern-jowled professors, to pass the hours before one can call it decently 'a day' and creep into bed at ten o'clock."   (October 12, 1953)

The "professors" in the last extract are a numerous folk in the repertoire of the late "doodlings." Outwardly, they are recognized by their gowns and mortarboards. They can be traced to June, 1952, when my father attended the Commencement Exercises at Sarah Lawrence College, where I had been teaching. The faculty were required to be present, garbed in the academic costume. Even though, in my case, the apparel was only rented and totally unadorned by any academic honors, my father got a great "kick" out of seeing his youngest son so attired. The sight of us all, graduating students and teachers, roasting in the sun for two mortal hours on the platform, appealed to his sense of the ludicrous, always on the alert where professional costume, uniforms, official insignia, were suspected of disguising human frailties.

Beneath the surface, the professor drawings seem to have something to do with the perils of the intellectual life. From a batch of drawings, most of which have no written captions, I was able to cull three specimens whose title contained the word "idea." All three, characteristically, are couched in terms of colloquial speech, not to say slang. "What's the Big Idea?" is an example. "Get the Idea?" is another. One "gets the idea" that these guardians of knowledge are being accused by the artist of dealing perfunctorily or incompetently, not to say venally, with the treasure of cognition under their care.

Some of the carved and drawn apparitions "hark back" to very early times, to Lyonel Feininger's Comic Page "The Kin-der-Kids," designed in 1906 for the Chicago Sunday Tribune. The "Mysterious Pete" in the above letter refers to a character from this comic series, and another figure, "Cousin Gussie," was whittled out of wood in the last years in New York. Both deserve a word of explanation.

The pen style "Kin-der-Kids" series was an ambitious invention. Its grand theme was the circum-navigation of the world, by a group of runaway boys of contrasting temperaments, accompanied by a supernaturally intelligent Dachshund endowed with the gift of speech. Their vessel was a claw-footed bathtub, propelled by a robot Japanese "water-baby" whose feet beat the waves like the paddles of a stern-wheeler. The flight was from the boys' "Auntie Jim-Jams," who in her turn organized her "relief expedition," a kind of female Dona Quixote, gaunt, angular, yellow-faced but, although imbued with a true spirit of Quixoterie, lacking perhaps the amiability of the immortal knight; her own accompanying animal was a cynical cat. Her squire in the pursuit was "Cousin Gussie," the Good Boy, trotting, flying (in a balloon) and navigating in various vessels meekly by her side, but not without sotto-voce asides betraying a secret sympathy with the fugitives. It is he who figures in some of the photographs (p. 63), a tiny blue body all but squashed beneath a monstrous sky-blue hat. The object of the chase was to administer a dose of castor oil to the boys. The sworn purpose of the pursued was to escape this prophylaxis.

This adventure story abounds in symbols characteristic of the structure of a certain kind of fairy tale. For instance, the temperaments of the three boys are like the embodiments of the qualities of the traditional hero: the brainy "Daniel Webster," a kind of juvenile "professor," everlastingly studying his encyclopedia in the midst of natural disasters and gleaning valuable knowledge therefrom; "Strenuous Teddy," the strong boy (a caricature of Theodore Roosevelt), whose muscular fitness and agility helps the boys out of many scrapes; and the voracious "Piemouth," the child with the bottomless appetite, the stomach of the group, whose greed gets them into trouble but whose amazing swallowing ability also solves some difficulties; this trio is supplemented by the robot "Japansky" of inexhaustible energy, and accompanied by the sagacious dog–the "helpful animal" in terms of the folklore mythologist.

To this heroic-helpless crew, this composite Odysseus, appears at certain occasions the ghostlike "Mysterious Pete," himself a complex figure of multi-national origins. "Pete" is a warner, a messenger in times of stress; he manifests himself only at the peak of some threatening calamity, a rigid forefinger extended straight out, half pointing, half menacing; a piercing single eye glowing from under the brim of a slouched hat. This combination of Mercury and Wotan is swathed in a blanket from the bottom of which are dangling skinny legs draped in Indian leggings; but his hat is the classical "lid" of the German Wild Huntsman.

In my father's old age these visitants came back to him with the fire of youth, the "long-lost glow of adventure" unquenched. The plot of "The Kin-der-Kids" was never carried through to the end; disagreements between artist and publishers led to a premature termination of the contract. Could it be that he was about to try to settle for himself that old dispute between pursuer and pursued? In 1906 he had left the adventurers in mid-ocean, or else in the heart of Asia, I do not remember which. It will never be known now whether the medicine was finally to be swallowed or not. Neither can we find out whether the artist interpreted "Auntie's" obstinacy of intention to administer the hated purgation as essentially helpful (if benighted) or as purely vengeful. Perhaps the conflict contained in the adventure was insoluble. The dualism of the motif behind the pageant is perhaps the crowning symbol of this "argosy" whose flavor lingers behind when I recall the many hours I have spent, as a boy, looking at the slowly crumbling pages of the Chicago Sunday Tribune, now at their final resting place in the library of the Museum of Modern Art in the city of New York.

*

In those years–the mid-twenties–began the time of growing intimacy and companionship between my father and myself. It had become evident that we shared certain basic interests. Of his three sons I, although the youngest, was the first to conquer the English language and to converse with him in his native tongue. The interest in ships, and in model-yacht building and sailing became another bond. It began with a few weeks of the early summer of 1924, when my father and I formed a sort of exploratory advance guard in new territory. The place was the small fishing village of West-Deep on the Baltic, for the next ten years the annual summer resort of the family. The novelty of the experience was equal for both participants. Although I was then a "teenager" with few of the exasperating symptoms of this interesting age missing, the advantages of having a companion seem to have outweighed the drawbacks. In the following years the experiment of the two of us preceding the rest of the family was repeated. On long walks through the woods and along the beach, my father had begun to talk to me of his early times in America, a topic of the most absorbing interest to me.

These stories were to me romantic pictures: tales of New York harbor and its ships (and waterside ruffians), the building of the East-side "El," the inauguration of Brooklyn Bridge viewed from a Manhattan rooftop, trips to the Great Lakes, fishing expeditions with his father, parades of the "Grand Army of the Republic" of which my grandfather was a member. I did not know then what I know now—I mean that in listening and asking for more of these stories, I identified myself with the teller of them and that then and there a private "new glow" was being kindled, which cannot be the subject of these lines. But later meditation has shown me that the inner core, the meaning of these souvenirs was just their mysteriousness in the awareness of the narrator himself. He was as surprised at what they presented as the listener could possibly be. A boy thinks of his father as a static, full-fashioned being for whom to change would be treachery or disaster; but the father talking to his boy may be making the discovery of just this kind of a change: a "cosmic" one, that of having progressed from sonship to fatherhood. A situation of long ago, which had originally been merely picturesque, may reveal itself as having undergone a transmutation during the time it had lain buried in oblivion. In one of the last letters my father ever wrote to me he remembered these times himself and put his stamp of valuation on them:

"Your letter . . . cheered me up and brought up many old memories, and I am happy that you think of including some of your earliest impressions in your talk at the Mint Museum. You need not do so, but it is good, I am glad that you feel that way about them."   (November 29, 1955)

Of all the tales of long ago, the most haunting to me is an account of how he and his father had strayed into an unfamiliar part of the vicinity of Lake George with their fishing gear, and had come to a deep pool in the thickest woods toward sunset time. The water was glassy and black as ebony; a huge boulder emerged half from the shore, half from the water, and opposite, the ranks of trees were impenetrable. The effect was awesome. His father made a cast into the pool and forthwith brought up a huge and monstrous eel, struggling fiercely. This apparition so increased the sense of something uncanny that they left the place without making another cast. A flavor of flight from a haunted spot attaches to the sudden departure, perhaps rationalized by a remark such as "It is getting late, we ought to be on our way."

How could this story fail to remind me of one of the artist's principal figurative themes, the angler! In watercolors, woodblocks, and oils, and in carved toys as well, the quays of harbors and the beaches of the ocean are thronging with fishermen. From another of the early stories one may gather how deeply rooted was the impression of fishermen that the artist had formed in his youth. A trip to South Carolina in 1879 with his mother, for the purpose of visiting his grandparents who were then living in Columbia, S.C., had left an image of certain "dark and enigmatic figures outlined against the shining water of a canal at sunset time," seen from the train as the travellers approached their destination. This view of Negroes trying for catfish (as he told me) remained the outstanding memory of an occasion which must have been momentous in other respects.

Rarely the main topic of a composition, the fishermen are there, in many pictures, ready to try their luck. The noteworthy exception to the reduced compositional function is the painting of 1912 and its replica of the same year, "Angler with Blue Fish" (Nos. 67 and 68 in the *œuvre* catalog of his paintings). The tense, ecstatic gesture of the lucky fisherman reverberates through the structure of the composition: the hurrying, vertical waves, the rune-like arabesques of the smoke of the steamer, the significant glow surrounding the immense three-decker in the roadstead as though it were summoned forth by the display of the blue fish. It is indeed a rare catch. Its color may be likened to the blue of the violin in the "Red Fiddler," another one of Lyonel Feininger's most pondered and symbolical compositions. The early appearance of the fish in his painting career may be interpreted as an augury of success for the labors and exertions which were to follow, and of which the many subsequent fishing figures are metaphors. A priceless fish which, once caught, can never be lost again.

The flow of memory cannot be directed backward for long without producing souvenirs of model-yacht building and sailing. Although they are not, strictly speaking, toys, I cannot leave them out entirely. Their design and construction illustrate that side of his personality which constitutes the counterpart to fantasy: precision, rational thought, planning. No doubt he would have agreed to my interpretation of their function. The sailing of the boats also presents a view which I wish to develop a little: the outdoor view of him, exerting himself at the oars, trying to keep up with the "little devils." There is a fine sense of companionship contained in the story of these few years. Even biographically the sport has its meaning. It was a "true love," the course of which had not run smoothly in his youth. My grandfather had the notion that "undue" preoccupation with precision was "inartistic." In my father's boyhood the old gentleman had tried to drum a little artistic sense into him by drumming the "tinkering" out. In this, I am happy to say, he did not succeed. As stated in the letter below, the decree forbidding further indulgence in model-yacht sailing was withdrawn as arbitrarily as it had been imposed. But the "boy Leo" survived these inconsistencies without material damage.

But the greatest interest to me lies in the operation of the sense of time:

". . . let me commence with a mention of the happy hours I spent with little Tomas [his first grand-son, son of Andreas] last Sunday afternoon at the Central Park Model Yacht Pond. Yes! after a pause of nearly fifty-six years I found myself once more attending to the needs of a little model yacht, with Tomas nominally in charge. *He* was interested; I do not know what to call my own reactions which were of a composite order . . . I had to recall your and my sailings in Deep . . . and how often we spoke of sailing one day on the lake in Central Park if we should ever get to New York . . . and how we not once came together near the Park and by the same token, never sailed our models together . . . Well! the sport is no longer what it was, in the 80s . . . when the three captains (Arvidsen, the Swede . . . silent, scraggly-bearded and grey . . .; Captain Grant, the American, also bearded and . . . the engineer and scientist of the group; and Tarleton, the Englishman and gentleman yachtsman) . . . brought out their newest creations . . . copies in miniature (exact as to all measurements) of the celebrated big yachts . . . the schooners 'Sappho,' 'Grayling' and 'Dauntless,' the cutters and sloops contending for the 'America's' Cup in 1885, 1886 and 1887! . . . the lovely rigs of them! in the days before yachting became an abstraction . . . I was in constant attendance, for at that time I had been taken out of school, being thought to be delicate in health, which I surely was not. . . But Time being what it is, does fly, and here I am, with my grandson at the Pond, and a heap of old memories for further company."

(April 4, 1943)

From 1925 to about 1932 the "annual Christmas craze" for making toys was equalled by a "spring craze" for devising and building new models for the summer at the seaside. These were built to *sail* (not, as has been alleged, to serve as "models" for paintings), and all ornamentation or attempt at duplicating in miniature the details of real vessels was left out. No railings, no fidded topmasts, nor even rudders were carried. For a sail-operated rudder to function properly the model yacht should

be as large as possible, certainly not under three feet in length, whereas my father's and my boats ranged from between 18 to 24 inches of waterline length. For windward work a model boat does not require a rudder, and all our sailing was of this kind, which made rowing after the boats a hard task. In designing I hotly competed with my father, but in execution his vastly greater skill and patience were "hors de concours" for me; my ambition to win pleased him and in many letters he is proud when he can announce the success of one of my boats. Here is a picture of what it was like:

". . . a North-west gale is howling over the land and thick layers of clouds are massed in the sky . . . in the afternoon, to the river, to sail model yachts. We were hardly out in the open and had the boats in the water, when a heavy rain squall came down; we took shelter in the reeds, the wind was tearing at our boat, but the models were sailing like witchcraft, much faster than we could follow with rowing . . . the outdoor exercise is good for us, we are always hungry. I am beginning to look like a human being once more." (August 22, 1926)

Another letter has something to say about the relationship of rational design and creative effort. The comparison he makes of boat-building and painting is surely enlightening in regard to his attitude toward his own potential:

"I am working, but worse than ever before. If, in former years, I could not help producing poor work at times, it was still dictated by enthusiasm and self-confidence–whereas now the entire being of Feininger is nothing but a question mark and one great doubt . . . this too will pass, of that I am convinced . . . Lux and I were out repeatedly in the rowboat on the Rega with the model yachts.

My boats are very successful this year. I have managed at last to design not only fast hulls, but to improve sailplans and the cutting of sails sufficiently to bring them up to modern standards ... I only wish I were painting thus well, but that will come ...."   (July 24, 1928)

The "modern standards" of which he speaks were the marconi rig with its characteristic tall, narrow, triangular mainsail cut with very little "belly." This rig, carried with minor modifications by large as well as by small yachts in the 20s and 30s, represents the "abstraction" of which he spoke in the 1943 letter of old sailing memories. If the poet in my father regretted the passing of the old and spectacular sailplans, the engineer in him could rejoice in the success of his design: it *worked* as a design should do. In this example of bowing, not unregretfully, to modern conditions (duplicated, by the way, in his marine compositions of this period), he gives us a foretaste of the later adjustment to contemporary New York.

*

In the preceding pages I have indicated to what an extent the last years in America were responsible for the toys and drawings forming the pictorial material of this book. My father's reactions to aspects of this momentous return to his native city shed valuable light on the creative process underlying his late work. As a study of this adjustment, not a biographical sketch, it is proper to accompany the artist on his final crossing of the Atlantic. To be sure we have already been in New York and have temporarily retraced our steps, as was dictated by the forward and backward motion of the time sense. Nor does this movement cease with my father's settling in Manhattan. But the values are reversed: the American in Germany, remembering the land of his birth, is replaced by the "German artist" in America, trying to get his spiritual no less than social and economic bearings.
This reversal, despite its superficial nature, threatened at first to become a real obstacle to his re-orientation, which is not surprising in view of the growing animosity in the United States toward things German at the time. But he saw clearly where the problem was and what its solution must be eventually:

"I no longer feel a pang when I am alluded to as the 'German painter.' I did truly suffer from the feeling of strangeness, at first. Now I only feel the urge in back of my work, of a tremendous advantage gained abroad."   (June 27, 1939)

Of the causes, as well as the means, of the actual return it does not seem necessary to say much. It may be of greater interest to learn something about my father's feelings toward Germany. If he had found it difficult to take sides in the First World War, this was not true for the second one. His innate pessimism had not changed, and he foresaw little good to come from the results of the world-wide upheaval; but he was unwaveringly certain that Nazism had to be destroyed. On the other hand he was able to distinguish between "Germany" and "Nazism," and there was too much rectitude as well as real understanding in him to permit his judgment to be clouded by hatred of a political régime. What was happening in the Germany of Hitler seemed to be almost as much an expression of the potential wickedness and folly of humankind at large as of a particular nation.

Two letter extracts will illustrate his post-war attitude:

"We are arranging the material at the gallery for my impending show in Germany. . . I am most . . . happy that the show will come off–it is a 'Rechtfertigung' [vindication] of a sort, and really a 'Danksagung' [demonstration of gratitude] toward many friends over there."   (May 27, 1954)

"From Germany come superlative criticisms of the show in Munich. Above all, they are personally conceived in 'Herzlichkeit' [cordiality]; the headings all stress that it is a 'Wiedersehn' [meeting again] with Feininger. And there is a willingness to make good for past indecisions . . ."
                                                                            (September 30, 1954)

There is a fitness in the circumstance that Munich was the host town for this exhibition, for in that same city the Nazis had staged, in 1937, their famous show of "degenerate art" in which my father was proud to figure.

But we are far ahead in our survey of the "conquest of New York." The first of the letters from which I am quoting may be viewed as closing an initial period. Perhaps the disappointment could have been predicted:

87

"For almost two years after our arrival here it seemed like a fairy tale... that I should actually be treading once more the old flagstones of my youth–until I finally gave up being only disillusioned in my unceasing attempts at re-discovering my native haunts. There is today scarcely a corner of Berlin and suburbs, ... where I have not more vivid feelings of home. Strange. Over there lies a graveyard of recollections, and here I am all alone in my native town, which scarcely anyone I meet seems to have known."

(April 21, 1943)

Until a certain, dramatic turning point arrived (we shall hear of it in its place), my father lived a fairly secluded life. His sons were dispersed through various countries "for the duration." Besides an occasional "movie," the chief recreation consisted in excursions through the city in company with my mother. A war-time picture in which the present mingles curiously with the past is conveyed by the letter which follows. As happens so often in my father's writings, his evocations of times gone by breathe a note of prophecy.

"... yesterday, on South Street, about eleven o'clock of a cloudless day, the view of the skyscrapers to the West against the deep tender blue of the sky was heartbreakingly lovely, because I could never hope to live long enough to do it justice in painting... And the river was aflame with reflections

88

and glitter, and hulking Liberty and Victory steamers, crammed full with turrets and heavy guns against the nazi submarines blocked out the shore opposite and made me long to reconstruct the old-time rows of tall, slender square-riggers . . . At the last pier before reaching South Ferry there were in line, one behind the other, two huge, dark red ferry boats, each with two big smokestacks and massed high as houses above the shed, showing two long rows of windows closed blindly to the light, in winter dry-dock . . . Vast spaces, empty, clean . . . in the old days the place was choked with all kinds of vehicles and the sounds were Babel; the iron-shod wheels and the horses' hooves created a din to split the ear and the cries of the hawkers filled the air . . . the cobblestones made walking a rough task; they were wet and slippery with refuse, littered with debris, old crates, cluttered with barrels and boxes, rotting fruit rests, dead cats, etc. But on the waterside, in stately rows, *stood the ships* with their bowsprits stretching almost into the windows of the houses opposite . . ."

(November 25, 1943)

The jump from "dead cats" to clipper ships is so essentially "Feininger" that at the risk of provoking the wrong kind of a laugh it must be underlined. The irony of the juxtaposition lies in the fact that ships, with their beauty and their romance, come and go in this world, and only the everyday litter remains; the pitiful object which is a dead cat is seen to have more lasting power than the stateliest ship and is thus a metaphor of the "live dog" of the parable; and my father lived to see the truth of it.

Besides the emotional adjustment, a professional and economic standing was to be secured. It was not an easy process and cost endless patience and fortitude. The first years were spent in a state of near poverty. What pills the aging artist had to swallow!

"Miss A. H. sent me a letter yesterday, returning all the photos and reproductions of paintings, regretting their being too 'subtle' for the new PM readers. Do you realize that this means some sort of reprimand? . . . I have been trying to imagine what might happen to PM if they actually did risk publishing one of my things . . ."   (June 27, 1940)

PM was an afternoon paper, first published in 1939, to serve the more intellectually-minded, generally liberal and "pro-New Deal" portion of the New York population. Considerable hopes had been attached to the newspaper's declared policy of giving coverage to contemporary movements in the arts.
My father's meditations on the differences between East and West produced a piece of great insight and self-criticism, stating an essential aspect of his art and defining his attitude toward his creations; he wrote to me:

"You are fortunate in finding genuine if somewhat intellectual appreciation for your work. I myself am often distressed at the emotional or even sentimental approach of some admirers of my work; and, taking it all in all, I am suspicious of the capacity for just appraisal of some of the best of these folks. Just what my work contains of the Remote is quite past . . . Americans; in fact, it constitutes a great hindrance to success here. 'Exhibitionism' is the great vogue now. I am at pains to retire behind my work, and there lies the difficulty . . ."   (July 11, 1940)

The next letter illustrates the difference in the economics of modern art then and now. It also portrays his will to endure in the face of obstacles.

"I have good news again; yesterday, two very pleasant and enthusiastic letters from the Museum in San Diego; one, announcing the sale to the museum (at my reduced rates) of two watercolors for $125.00; and the other, telling me that a watercolor at the exhibition in San Diego had received the

'Honorable Mention.' This so delighted the director, Dr. Poland, that he wrote a most cheery letter to me about it, whilst giving a graphic description of how money-less the museums now are . . . the purchasing committee . . . regretted that they could buy only two of the drawings; but asked whether I could consider 'rounding out the sale' by dedicating a third drawing to the collection, to be permanently hung in the museum. . . I think that, in this case, the drawing Poland asks for (a small abstract ship, listed at $50.00) will contribute well towards giving a good group with the two others, and will be well placed; better than lying unseen and uncared-for in one of my scrapbooks at home. So I'll place it on the 'publicity budget' . . ."   (June 25, 1941)

These are the years when his outlook was changing in favor of today, away from an everlastingly elusive yesterday. That he could watch the removal of that old and treasured landmark, the Second Avenue "El," is more than remarkable; it is symbolical of a new departure. He wrote that it was to stop running in June and that it was to be taken down shortly afterward.

"When we return to the apartment in the fall, there will be no curve any more at 23rd Street and no blessed squealing when the trains negotiate the narrow and ungreased radius . . ."   (May 24, 1942)

His windows, although on the 11th floor, were right above this curve; and the noise of trains on the three-track system during rush hours had been deafening. Still! I think that it indicates the same spirit as the next quotation: that the gain is greater than the loss of what had to be given up. The letter below is another one of those written during rather lonely times in the city largely emptied of friends because of the war, a description of a walk "after hours" with my mother:

". . . we turned at 64th Street in Central Park and spent a happy hour with the animals. Above all, the great outdoor cage of macaws and parakeets was bemusingly beautiful; we all know, and have known since earliest childhood, how vivid in color these Brazilian and Australian birds are, but one has to see them again . . . to fully grasp the fact of their glory. It is the same with those rainbow-hued exotic fishes; it is uplifting to see them now and then. . . The most of us forget what glory there is in Creation, in our measly grubbing scrabblings for daily survival in towns. I don't want here to belittle anyone's appreciation of beauty; but Oh my! how much we are missing for [the sake of] drab and sordid interests and how we allow them to take full possession of our routine existence . . ."   (May 30, 1942)

We now arrive at the *coup de théâtre* which was to change my father's professional standing. He met with composure a change for the better of his fortunes so sudden that it might have turned the head of a man less tried and proven by adversity.

It happened in two days, fortunately for us fully described by him in letters:

". . . yesterday I went to the 'Varnishing' (as they persist in calling it) of the new exposition of American Painting at the Metropolitan Museum, having one of my paintings included . . . Dr. Lilienfeldt brought it there himself, . . . although (not being 'in the know' I had not been invited to exhibit) the limit for delivery had already passed. It is a show to demonstrate the Victory of the American Artist, and when pictures (3000 of them) have gone through the process of being juried, and 300 chosen and hung, and shown to the good old public, there is a second jury to decide which paintings seem worthy of acquisition by the Metropolitan . . . well, there we have now a painting in the pool and a one-in-ten-thousand chance that it might be acquired . . . Gosh, was I discouraged when . . . I caught a glimpse of all the folks milling around . . . but I did discover my 'Gelmeroda' (now modestly designated under the caption 'Church'), hung very nicely . . . probably I am all wrong but it looked to me to be still a pretty good painting; but, as far as the frame was concerned, it lacked that impressiveness, being but a silver, wedge-shaped, delicate profile of my own designing, some twenty years ago . . . still, nobody seemed to object, for no one even glanced at the picture except (for a period of three seconds during which I held my breath) a stout, unstylish-looking leddy [sic] in a red hat . . . to return for a moment to the misleading term: 'Varnishing Day'. . . let smile who will at my innocence, I, before leaving the apartment to proceed to the ordeal . . . took care to wrap up a bottle of varnish in a clean white piece of linen bedsheet and conceal a brush in the depths of the pocket of my winter coat, just not to take any chances . . ."   (December 6, 1942)

He had thought "in his innocence" that *vernissage* still meant what it used to mean, ages ago, in Paris, the day before the public opening of an exhibition of paintings, when artists had an opportunity to refresh their canvases with a touch of varnish. He had not wanted to be unprepared,

92

in case it should be called for. The painting does not seem to have required touching up, doing very well without it:

"It has been a hectic day. At 9:30 a. m. I was painting . . . and my thoughts dwelt gloomily on 'Pearl Harbor' and what this day meant in America's and the world's history when suddenly the doorbell rang . . . I went to the door . . . and without stood a letter-carrier extending a registered letter. So I signed the receipt and looked at the sender . . .: Metropolitan Museum . . . – H'm, thinks I–I held the letter playfully out to Mami and gave her 'three guesses.' First, she guessed 'Lux,' then 'Andreas,' then she gave up guessing. . . I then proceeded to open it and on revealing its contents I nearly fell on my 'back-porch' (or do only girls have these?) . . . a check for $2,500.00 lay in my hand, *tout comme ça* . . . the telephone calls . . . immediately began to hail upon us. – It is a good old American saying that 'Nothing succeeds like success.' – At 11, I had regained my accustomed imperturbability and was painting as usual (using a ruler) when for the 'steenth time the telephone rang, and this time . . . for me, from the Metropolitan. I received the nicest invitation to an informal luncheon with the Director and others . . . *j'ai accepté avec empressement*. And now, after three-and-a-half hours of the most hectic, *me voilà enfin*. – The luncheon was given in the secret recesses of the Museum *souterrain*, in a very cosy room; and there may have been some 100 people present . . . the lunch was crowned by . . . a delicious cigar, 'La Corona, Belvederes,' of which I surreptitiously preserved the ring for my records . . . the Director made an announcement that the guests were please to quit eating at 2:45 on account of the impending official solemnities at which HIZZONER, the Little Flower [Mayor Fiorello La Guardia] was to give an address. . . Hell! at our table all four gents were smoking these plusquamperfect Coronas when the signal . . . was given . . . with heavy sighs we went forward . . . at 3 p.m. the attendants began to get nervous, the director, Dr. Taylor, drew his gold repeater and chain repeatedly, ladies in charge of various official duties hostessing began to corrugate their brows and look important WHEN, before one saw him, HIZZONER was on the steps leading to the sacrosanct improvised scaffold and a deep breath of relief shook the official bosoms, and the speech-making was on . . . the Mayor . . . sat more or less at ease . . . and twisted his face into divers shapes and looked utterly unconcerned. But he spoke . . . much to the point. No artist . . . but felt that . . . here was a man who did not think that an artist was a moron if he kept on sculpting or painting when better, perhaps brawnier, men were knocking Nazis on the noodle. In fact he made it clear that now, JUST

NOW, was the time to keep the good ol' lamp alight. There was a lot of cheering when he ceased and people liked him a lot. So do I, for one . . . all the time I was sitting in the hall I could see the ever-lovely Victory of Samothrake placed at the head of the stairs . . . eternal as art itself. . . Many acquaintances congratulated me, colleagues, art dealers, I was honestly touched by such evidence of liking and good-feeling. And if I wrote yesterday that no one (except the lady in the red hat) even cast a glance at my poor painting, today it was quite something different! There was a big brass shield fastened on the frame of each prize-winner, and all the nice people were looking out hungrily for those brass shields and where they saw such a one, they just stood in crowds to read the name of the artist and the amount of . . . the prize. And, by degrees, some even came to look at the picture itself. . . Gosh, dear old son, it was a happy day today . . ." (December 7, 1942)

With this event we have seen the last of the several changes from seclusion into public life of which I have spoken earlier. The painter had come into his own. Society having ceased to withhold its reward–having, indeed, made up for past hesitancies with a lavishness truly "American"–the artist had now fully entered into his productive and vigorous "late period." How energetic and self-reliant are these lines:

". . . when we do go out it is astonishing how little it takes to please us, and at that it is almost exciting: the color of the pale lavender sky over and beside a group of sunlit tall buildings with one slashing black shadow across the multi-bewindowed acres of wall . . . New York is a marvellous place and yet almost all the paintings I have seen of N.Y. motifs look stale and 'abgedroschen' [trite] . . . there should be a way, if one could free oneself from the superabundance of material, detail, the too obvious clap-trap. It seems to me the city should be divested of all episodical by-work . . . one picture I want to paint is the East River from our windows, some day. That is an enchanting subject, above all on a misty, grey day, like yesterday and today . . ." (March 31, 1943)

The eyes and the mind being open to the world that *is*, it is not surprising to read:

"Suddenly I can handle color without difficulty once more . . . a couple of weeks ago I finished two or three new paintings . . . one, a marine, showing two *Schärenkreuzer* [marconi-rigged yachts] in the middle distance, one standing in towards the observer, the other (on the left side of the pix) in slender profile against a deep-brown barque in the background, and the whole composition against an ultramarine blue coast under a greyish-green clouded sky. This painting was, so to speak, taken right from the easel and quickly framed and transported to the current show of 'Modern Trends in Painting' at the Puma Gallery where it now hangs. Another painting . . . is about the jolliest bit of color I've put on canvas . . . It is painted very smudgily, the colors being extended beyond the forms of the houses, but with fine, sharp and precise lining in black and white contours. Gosh! there's brown and greyish-yellow, brick-red, greyish-green, dirty-white (with grey smudges of color in the midst): and, on the ground, pure Veronese green and, in the greyish-green sky, Zinc yellow. How's that . . .?"   (February 20, 1944)

The marine painting he described in the letter above combines the new and the old in juxtaposing the modern yachts with the old brown square-rigger which he saw and sketched in 1910 and 1911 from the beach of Heringsdorf on the Baltic. The barque was a regular trader from Norway to the port of Swinemuende, making fortnightly trips, and a snapshot of her with the artist gazing up at her rigging appears amongst the illustrations. I am quoting from one more letter to complete the picture of the Here and Now.

"For the summer I have well-defined plans: I intend to make a series of 'Manhattan' compositions to be painted during next winter . . . some . . . old buildings in Lexington Avenue I have long considered as a subject–these buildings are almost uniform in height and style and cover two blocks and are utterly uninteresting, considered as architecture . . . just this monotony is what gives me the idea, for viewed in perspective, they form a continuous 'cliff,' rhythmically perforated with window-openings in 4 storeys, but–and here's the rub!–each house is a different shade of brown, grey, soot, with two or three nearly white ones in between just where they form an exciting series of vertical fields, blending or contrasting along the entire length of the two blocks. Certainly, within their individual limits there are interesting divergencies of detail–for instance, one group of 2 or 3 houses has arcades on the ground storey, which look positively beautiful if considered as architectural 'understatement.' Certain shop signs . . . also give accents–but first and foremost is the impression of a two-block sweep of *cliff* . . ."   (June 8, 1944)

To appreciate the gradually changing tone of these communications one must have known the difficulties which had to be overcome before my father could bring himself even to try to paint in his small apartment. It is the contrast of the beginning with the present state of mind that causes me to think of these years as the crowning triumph of his will to overcome handicaps contained as much in his intimate make-up as in external circumstances. For years to come, doubts, frustrations and disappointments are absent from his letters.

The process of adaptation which I have documented with letters by the artist and which I have designated as the "conquest of New York" appears to me to be the result of protracted efforts of the will. There is little doubt in my mind that Lyonel Feininger was to some extent aware that the first years of his life in America presented a problem of sink or swim. He must have sensed that the roads behind him were blocked; he had to go forward or perish.

We have seen that he did go forward, and we have had glimpses of what he felt during the process, and what comforts he found within himself and in the world. The irony underlying his success at the "Artists for Victory" exhibition cannot have escaped the reader. Was the success any more rational than the previous lack of it? Did it make any more sense? No: will and reason had done their best, and they had done it very well. But their's were not the only voices he could hear. There was something else, barely touched by success or failure. Another force was active and could be perceived in the life of the spirit as well as in the incomprehensible workings of the social-economic body. That dark other world of the "Remote" did not own itself beaten by the ascendancy scored by the Will.

It is not a simple task to approach reasonably a theme which is by definition the opposite of reasonable. Predilection, whim, personal value, associative appeal—by what laws are these governed? Are they even governed at all? When exploring these forces, do we not grope in darkness, and do not the signs and apparitions which we do behold, owe their light which is fitfully illuminating them, to a source not under our control? The old artist has gained a command over his visual means which may seem wizard-like to the spectator. But where are the fire, the love of adventure which does not count the cost, the foolish fine enthusiasm of the early times of exploration? Old age comes to us all; but it comes in different guise for each of us. One does not stem decay; but the oak and the reed each have "virtue" in them and the wise old man is he who knows when to be one or the other. The will to create, to continue, to produce, can only do so much; when it flags, falters, comes to a standstill, let other powers speak. When the sense of life has withdrawn, the richest display of colors, the most pondered and balanced piece of design, the bulging sketchbooks of the past, are as nothing. In such a state–familiar to all artists–the smallest, meanest bit of significant reality outweighs all the empty flourishes of a craft

not guided by inspiration. To use my metaphor of the Harbor Walk: any "dead cat" is preferable to the uninspired exercises of mere skill.

This is the wisdom and the greatness of Lyonel Feininger's late life: having stood up stiffly to the winds of adversity, he knew when to yield with humility to the gale of passionate experience. Experience of what? What else but life, existence with all that may imply? The greatness also lies in knowing how to refrain from attaching preconceived values to "messages" not man-made.

A pair of letters, written at an interval of less than two months, will illustrate my meaning.

"In the evenings I do truly enjoy commencing some sketch or other, to be worked out in the light of day. Mostly droll figures, I must say, whereby I have an opportunity to go into coloring, brightly . . . I have done some photography with color film here . . . I chiefly enjoyed those yellow hydrants with red tops and black outlets. . . This, at any rate, is pure color. What I really miss is drawing after nature, making 'Notizen' [sketches] as at the Baltic, in Deep, or in the villages in the vicinity of Weimar. Somehow I have no satisfaction from the subjects hereabouts; they form too little of my own, inner preference and only result in naturalistic efforts."   (October 6, 1953)

This letter, written ten years after the discovery that "New York is a marvellous place" to paint, expresses the ebbing of the tide; the current was running in the opposite direction. Neither the available scenery, nor the images of memory alone, could produce the spark. In his search for he did not know what, he had come upon the hydrants.

I cannot say exactly when he began to collect color shots of the hydrants, but it was around the time the first "droll figures" appeared. Sketching at Plymouth (despite his real fondness for the place) produced only "naturalistic effort," hence did not interest him. It was not what was wanted. But the hydrants had "pure color." Their appeal was comparable to the "uplifting effect" the tropical birds and fishes had had for his eye. It makes no difference whether God, Nature or Man applies the color, so long as the eye may behold it. And let it be "pure," that is to say, not tainted by descriptive purpose.

The haddock is a fish as well as the angelfish; a sparrow no less a bird than the macaw. But the artist is not looking for the quiddities of birds and fishes, but of color. Yellow, red and black on a hydrant in Plymouth county means that this township is responsible for this piece of equipment. Much the painter cares about that! It is the color he wants, it is the color he needs to see: and when they come into his field of vision (not before) he recognizes that this is what he had been missing. This is what I had in mind by speaking of "humility." The search for the consonance of light and space had at the present moment led to a piece of gaily colored hardware unexpectedly rearing up at a dusty roadside.

It does not require a great effort of the imagination to see such a hydrant, perhaps half concealed by a clump of New England weeds, as resembling in all essentials one of the brightly-colored "droll figures," "ghosties," or "professors." What is perhaps a little more surprising is to learn that, besides

114

containing the water pressure specified by local fire department regulations, these installations should have been the dispensers of the Waters of Life.

". . . a painting I made on chrome yellow ground two weeks ago is traceable to the gaudy Plymouth hydrants. . . On a yellow ground tone the village of Gaberndorf (near Weimar) with the church steeple in the background over the gables of the houses in the foreground. The sky, painted thinly on the strong yellow, is a very pale prussian blue mixed or deadened with terre verte; the roofs are all bright orange vermilion red, the church spire with a *Zwiebelturm* [bulb-base spire] is light cobalt violet and a part in red. The tree foliage in the upper right of the picture–of course in abstract triangles-- is rubbed in with a loose net of charcoal strokes on yellow. That is the entire color scheme, painted on burlap with the grain strongly marked and the drawing all in charcoal lines without any attempt at concealing this unorthodox medium. The effect is rich; the partly rubbed-in charcoal gives a warmth to the yellow in the house walls which is to be compared with an ancient Chinese painting on gold . . . well, you'll see it and laugh . . ."   (November 29, 1953)

The term "color synthesis" has been in use since the time of Cézanne to describe a particular handling of subject-matter and color and would also characterize, in a technical sense, the painting of which we have just read. But I should like to extend the word beyond its technical and historical limits. How much more than color-forms has come together here! The Thuringian Village, a New England Town, painted in New York; the 1910s and the 1950s; a nature sketch and almost pure invention–by way of the vision of an antiquated piece of ironmongery in gay colors. But these elements do not complete the count, indeed they would mean but little without that supreme "synthesis," or putting together of two contrasting modes of outlook: will and inspiration, the endurance of the oak and the bending of the reed. The red, yellow and black hydrant of Plymouth responsible for the painting of Gaberndorf is as disparate an element as the peacock was in the village half-way up the Ettersberg. What I find most impressive in this letter, however, is the spirit of analysis penetrating the complex workings of the creative process. This speaks of self-knowledge, of the same kind as the labors of the soul produced in the "conquest of New York." The state of mind which could create the work and trace it to the origins speaks of integration, a symbol of which is the *coniunctio oppositorum.*

In my father's last letters, intimations of this dynamism occur more frequently than before. The passages dealing with trees may have foreshadowed this intuitive equating of life and art. He comes still closer to absolutes when he writes, not only as a father to a son, but as one painter to another:

"Today I am doing for the first time in months what I truly hope and wish you may be happily doing in the spare hours allotted to you from teaching labors: *Painting* [his italics]; and that with a certain long-lost glow of adventure and eagerness. It has been a period such as I never have gone through before, of frustration and entire indifference to creative effort–even music had rarely an appeal, and my attention wandered, whatever I undertook.–Yes. I've been 'below par' in some mysterious lowering of mental efficiency . . . Now, old son, I am emerging in proper shape. Am also doing two lithographic stones of which I have hopes. It is good to write to you this rainy morning, *le gris clair* so conducive to retrospective effort . . ." (March 1, 1955)

By "absolutes" I mean the discovery of the relatedness of the "glow of adventure" to "retrospective effort." The creative moment moves freely in time and space. But there is the aging and weary body, the wandering attention. What could be more "cosmic" than the perception of the coming dissolution?

In the autumn of the same year, there are further expressions of a subliminal wisdom:

"This summer has shown me that there are such times in one's elder life when one retires deeply into the *néant* of emotion, into a dreamland which is soothing indeed . . ." (no month, 1955)

This is a generally human experience. It is a mercy shown to those who know how to bow to the inevitable. A more specific adaptation of the painter to the cosmic dynamism is portrayed in the following:

". . . I incline ever more to reduce my *Sprache* [language] in painting to the merest essences of line and color; as a Painter I am hopelessly bound even though I have an appreciation for the properties of pigments in using them in my sparse way. I am nearing a stage where I am even commencing to annihilate precise form, in the interest–as it seems to me–of unity. This is a precarious stage to enter into, and I am occasionally brought up short and revert to something contradictional as a corrective . . ."   (September 12, 1955)

In interpreting his pictorial procedure, does he not express perfectly the workings of a Larger Way, which likewise "annihilates precise form" (the human consciousness or identity) in the "interest of unity" (the Ultimate Union)?

A glow before it can be lost, must have existed, must have glowed. The discovery that once there had been a glow of "adventure and eagerness" *makes* the artist, constitutes the difference of temperament which distinguishes the painter and the poet from, let us say, the sailor or the hunter of big game. Is not art re-discovery? After all, we are all glad to be alive (even though we sometimes foolishly pretend that we are not, or that we were born too early or too late, or what not); none of us likes the creeping diminutions which the coming of old age imposes upon us; few of us face extinction with anything like deliberation. But we are not all artists. The studio, the writer's desk, the theatre, are workshops of the mind as well as of the hands; a transformation goes on there, the distilling of a quintessence of life, the raw materials of which were, to begin with, of an entirely private nature, meaningful only to the one to whom they came (whether sought or otherwise), but whose product becomes the property of thousands. The labors of the memory, of longing, of recall and evocation–briefly, of imagination–furnish the heat beneath the retort, the thrice-precious fuel consisting of elements of the spirit, the intellect, and the emotions. The artistic effort, the composing, destroying and re-building, fans the embers into the glow which, at the given moment looks like the real glow of the times gone by, but which, I speculate, may well exceed in heat, in light and in purity, the earlier one which had been "lost."

*

In attempting to sum up and to bring to a final conclusion the theme of toys and art, or of form and fantasy, or of whim and will, I find that once again the artist's own pen has furnished me with a vehicle. A letter written two months after the *coup de théâtre* with which his luck had turned early in the year, which was to bring his big two-man exhibition (with Marsden Hartley) at the Museum

118

of Modern Art (already scheduled at the time of writing), describes the lighter side of his life in those days:

"... but let me just tell about ... a reception and 'Buffet dinner' for a 'few artists and friends' of the Modern Museum [at the occasion of a preview of a retrospective International Drawing Exhibition] ... when we arrived, we were astonished to find the place crowded with the 'few friends and artists' – *Quatsch!* [nonsense] – few artists and other friends ... well, as I started out to say, we found quite a gay crowd already at the checking counter at 7:30 p.m. and when we were brought in the elevator to the main floor we were on the outskirts of a vast number of happily shouting, cheerful good people, each one balancing a mighty fine, large glass of Martini. The noise of their talking was simply shattering and it wasn't possible to understand a word of what was being said, but ... it sounded mighty festive. There were so many folks standing in front of the buffet where the drinx [sic] were being served, that we saw nothing ... of it, but in a very few minutes we were served ... each with a huge Martini brought forward by attentive butlers and presented with a smile of welcome from these good souls... We were met by chairmen and chairladies and introduced and made to feel at home, and spent a pleasant *quart d'heure* in the midst of the racket made by all the people attempting to make themselves heard, and we too did our darndest to swell the volume of shattering sound ... Then someone ... announced that dinner was about to be served on the Penthouse floor... At the end of the vast room dotted with cosey little round islands of tables and low, comfortable basketware armchairs, was the dinner buffet with about half a dozen young girls dishing out the eats and handing them to the teetering crowds waiting three deep ... later on, coffee was passed around by courteous Ganymaedchen ... don't ask me what we all talked about, for I don't remember but ... everything said or done seemed to be out of the ordinary and very pleasant, and everybody as nice and hearty as could be... After our coffee ... we went ... to the main floor where the Exhibition of Drawings was. Nobody, except for a few gallery officials, was downstairs, ... the whole magnificent show ... entirely undisturbed... The drawings commenced with the Impressionists: grand old names! Cézanne, Seurat, Toulouse-Lautrec, Degas, Rodin, Monet, Manet, Pissarro, Renoir– and went along with the historical development, right to the artists of our own days. French, Americans, Germans, Russians, Italians–we've never seen a more fascinating collection ... in the last of the long row of rooms, together with Picasso, Klee and others of the 'Abstractionists' hangs a pen-drawing of mine . . . 'Viaduct' . . . it is a good drawing, but I could have sent at least as good, preferably a charcoal or two. But it was satisfying to find myself in such . . . company." (February 20, 1944)

Small blame to the old gentleman for celebrating this once a golden moment! He must have felt inspired by more than the "huge Martinis": besides the forthcoming big show at the Museum, he had a most successful exhibition on the walls of the Curt Valentin Gallery at the time of writing. His very appreciation of the "drinx" speaks of the essential sobriety of his everyday life. As to the gentle fun poked at the "good souls" feasting above, with never a one of them paying any attention to the Masters downstairs, this is a theme we have encountered in the "Woman in an Exhibition" of 1908. But this time it is self-criticism, made in a spirit of common sinnership. He admits to having enjoyed the vinous confabulation.

This scene, when I came across it in my sheaf of my father's letters, irresistibly called up, not just one drawing, but the entire collection of grotesques, whether carved or drawn. In the presentation of this crowd, where everybody has his or her say, where nobody listens and where the din is too great to understand a syllable even if one were listening, very cheerful and presumed hopefully to be good-natured, I sense something like the elemental quality of the "Praise of Folly." It would be doing the little drawings a great injustice to be too literal. We have, here and there, made some such essay, without, I hope, too much hampering free play of imagination. But now is the time for a general last look. The "messages" are obviously made with the intention of presenting something humorous, even cheerful. One is invited to laugh, not so much *at*, as *with* the apparitions. But it is also evident that there is something underneath the mostly gay plumage. The colorful throng executes its capers in the Penthouse, above the galleries where the drawings or images are waiting.

I have said before that the "messages" are not all titled, although virtually all of them are signed and dated. The signature is sometimes (not often) humorously rendered as "Leinoel Einfinger" (read: Linseed Oil One-Finger), a play on sound based on accidental misspellings of the artist's name half a century earlier. But where there are titles, they resemble the misspelled signature. They are apt to be unenlightening, often slangy, exclamatory, intentionally misspelled or phonetically rendered, sometimes in French or German. One is forced to conclude that inscriptions form part of the disguise of the "message" and have not the function of clarifying the meaning of the picture. Perhaps the contrary? In any case, my survey of more than a hundred of these trilingual syllabifications suggested to me something like the "Buffet Supper at the Museum" as the common theme of them all–that is to say, a humanistic critique of society in the modern language of the pictograph. Imaginative as these drawings and carvings are, they are not in themselves the final images but they stand in front of, or above them. The galleries for the inauguration of which the crowd has been assembled, are elsewhere and have not yet been seen. They never will quite be seen in this life. They are the cave where the *Eidolon* is housed. The entire collection of grotesques is a Dance of Death. The particular aspect of any unit forming part of the cycle may be "harmless" or the opposite, but in their totality, the grotesques are all stating the same truth, are laughing or gritting their teeth at the same finding: Existence exists.

*

Ten years after the Museum party, my father wrote me another letter, again recording the labors and emotions that had gone into the preparation and attention required by an exhibition at the Curt Valentin Gallery. A peaceful mood is conveyed by the lines:

". . . we've had two and a half days of torrential downpour–something we've been praying for and at which, when it happens, we have only dirty words to sling! or? – at any rate, I love it! – it capsules my world into misty atmosphere, intriguing half-lights. I've got really nothing against New York either, as I've been slowly realizing. Except that it is too 'chuck-full' of subjects–and 'nuts' of course. But although I identify myself now to quite an extent with New York, it really is 'old New York,' the one of the Valentine's Manuals, I actually can be at home in: perhaps it does take 83 years to get that way! – . . . I have missed our personal writing these weeks, but I have been very tired after the show was done . . . the healing process . . . and then developing new directions as a consequence... was absorbing to the exclusion of sustained correspondence. Words are like acids sometimes; when a 'nartist' [sic] talks of what he is planning to do, they eat away the *fine fleur* of his *rêverie* . . ."

(May 21, 1954)

The synthesis is now complete. Integration is consummated because the writer knows and is able

121

to state, his position: "old New York" lives in him, as he lives in the New York of the moment. The conflict between the "fairy tale" of the lost city of his youth and the "marvellous city" which must be painted (and which was painted) has been resolved; he who never read Proust, has *retrouvé le temps perdu*.

The question of whether German or American can have meaning only if it adds to the understanding of Lyonel Feininger's art. Nationalities do not matter. Language and climate, both spiritual and atmospheric, do matter. Great art tells of a great soul. And he is great who has received and transmuted to a higher stage heritages of both East and West.

Parts of this work would have been impossible without the generous assistance of my mother, Mrs. Julie Feininger, and Dr. Charles Kuhn, Director of the Busch-Reisinger Museum at Harvard University, who both made letters and other materials relating to the subject of my father's toys available to me. I am also greatly indebted to Mr. William S. Lieberman, of the Museum of Modern Art in New York, for lending photographs of graphic works. More particularly, however, I wish to express my appreciation of his thoughtful and perceptive exhibition of 1963, "The Intimate World of Lyonel Feininger." Some of the leading ideas which I have used in my text first germinated in the presence of the works assembled in this show. But the greatest portion of my gratitude goes to my wife, Pat Randall Feininger. I thank her both for the encouragement she gave me, and for the criticism she did not spare me. Without the latter, the book would have fared ill; without the former, there might not have been a book at all.

Cambridge, October, 1964.

*

Concerning Lyonel Feininger's letters: As is known, the artist corresponded in several languages with many friends. In the interest of documentation, I am listing those letter extracts which have been quoted in the original language and text. Unless noted, all other letter passages have been translated by me. Extracts are listed by date, in chronological order.

Originals in English: April 20, 1914, January 9, 1937, September 12, 1938, June 27, 1939, June 27, 1940, July 11, 1940, June 25, 1941, May 24, 1942, May 30, 1942, December 6, 1942, December 7, 1942, March 31, 1943, April 4, 1943, April 21, 1943, November 25, 1943, February 20, 1944, June 8, 1944, July 2, 1946, September 12, 1953, October 6, 1953, October 12, 1953, November 1, 1953, November 29, 1953, May 21, 1954, May 27, 1954, September 30, 1954, October 29, 1954, November 5, 1954, December 5, 1954, December 29, 1954, March 1, 1955, no month 1955, September 12, 1955, November 29, 1955.